2.00/
Rich

The Flower of Grass

The Flower of Grass

EMILE CAMMAERTS

"For all flesh is as grass and all the glory of man as the flower of grass" (I PETER, I:24)

HARPER & BROTHERS PUBLISHERS

NEW YORK and LONDON

110903

239.U
C198

To my daughter

Jeanne Cammaerts

Contents

vii

Foreword

WHETHER ONE PERIOD OF HISTORY IS MORE OR LESS WICKED than another is known only to God, but each has its characteristic manifestations, its typical vice and virtue, and of the age which has just ended, at least in Europe, amid blood and screams, it may be said that it was honest but without honor. Again, it is wrong to speak of ages of faith and ages of doubt, as if a man could ever be without either, but each has its favorite idol, and of the late age it may be said that it had a belief, approaching superstition, in the presentational immediacy, the being-there-ness of a fact, and a doubt, approaching denial, of its having any further meaning or value.

In consequence, while other epochs produced fairy tales, heroic tragedies, fantastic comedies, i.e. imagined histories in which the probability of an event was subordinate to its importance as a link in a clear and closed pattern, the typical literary production of this one has been the diary, the true confession, the autobiographical novel, the column of off-the-record "personal" opinion, the day-to-day journalism of the self, i.e. a documentation as "factual" and without pattern as a telephone directory.

The writers of such works are, of course, guided, consciously or unconsciously, by some principle of selection. Behind some autobiographies, one senses the desire of their subject to prove that he or she is unique, "not like all those people over there," behind others a fear that unless his private experiences can arouse public interest, they may not be real, behind others the wish to confess

ix

and be forgiven, behind others again, a hope that the mere facts themselves, if only they are recorded accurately enough and in sufficient detail, will of themselves supply the pattern of meaning which the author seeks. So too with our pleasure in reading such documents. If someone admits to a sin of our own of which we have always been ashamed, we feel relieved, as if the mere fact that we are not unique made our guilt less; if someone enjoys or dislikes the same things as we do, we are reassured that our feelings are genuine. It is only in rare cases, of which Mr. Cammaerts' quiet warm record is one, that we find what probably we are always secretly hoping to find, and what alone justifies autobiographical writing, a life like our own but with the pattern of meaning in it disclosed, a carpet with a figure.

It is doubtful if an esthetically satisfying autobiography can be written except after a conversion to some kind of dogmatic belief which provides its subject with a fixed point from which to review his past life objectively as if it were that of a third person, for as long as truth is simply whatever the ego happens to observe about the self, the facts are infinite in number and there is no good reason why one should be more important than another; further, it is doubtful, I think, that it will then be written unless the conversion is to a belief in a personal God, for if the truth is an abstract idea like platonism or marxism, then the particular route taken by the individual to reach it is irrelevant; all that matters is the correct conclusion. Only a belief in a personal relation between an erring soul and a God of truth who is at all times concerned with that soul can make the history of its errors significant. Mr. Cammaerts' book, in fact, like those of St. Augustine and Cardinal Newman before him, is not so much an autobiography as a paragraph in the biography of the Divine Grace, a footnote in the ever-incomplete history of the acts of the Holy Spirit on this world. Such a note is necessarily documentary in method—poetic fiction is not history—and necessarily autobiographical in form, because it is within the subject that the eternal Word is made temporal flesh.

What has Mr. Cammaerts to report? He tells of a shy boy who is brought up on Rousseau by a gentle mother to whom he is devoted. He has an elder brother with whom he is close friends. He goes to school and is shocked by the rough and vicious behavior of the other boys. He flies to Nature for comfort only to find that Nature too is cruel. He goes to college and meets an inspiring teacher who is a fanatical socialist. He fails to become a socialist and the two become estranged. He begins a literary career. The first World War comes. Without any spectacular spiritual experience he becomes an Anglican though he doesn't go to church much. He gets married, very happily, to an English actress who goes to church. They move from Belgium to England. They have several children and the family is a united one. The second World War comes. One of his sons is killed. That is all. There are confessions, but not to any spectacular sins, only to having believed in quite ordinary idols, the beauty of Nature and the innate goodness of Man, to having felt superior to joining in public worship, to having been overly fussy about esthetic defects in churches, to having taken happiness too much for granted. Conflicts and sorrows are referred to in passing but no details are given. The author's career as a writer is not discussed at all. If, in the last war or in this, he took part in any exciting events, they are not described. The picture simply and honestly painted is of a life like many others, quiet, fairly successful and probably happier than most.

"Where is the story?" the journalist will ask, and the psychologist, "Where are the significant and fascinating details?" Just so. For Mr. Cammaerts is not trying to write their kind of book; he is not trying to amuse or startle, but to give evidence, to say enough and no more to make the reader understand what the witness could say in one sentence: "I was dead and am alive again; I was lost and am found."

For myself, it is the very ordinariness of his evidence that makes it convincing. When I first began reading St. Augustine, Pascal and Kierkegaard, I was, naturally, impressed that minds so infinitely more acute than mine should believe the Nicene Creed. Being most unwilling to accept what would call in question my whole way of life, I looked for a way out and for one whose generation was familiar with Freud, this was easy to find, for all three had obviously neurotic temperaments, aggressive desperate natures to whom life was always a foxhole under fire, and who had good reason to hate themselves. "For them," I argued, "the Christian faith was the natural, and in their day, probably the only solution to their abnormal situation. Indeed, from what I have seen of psychoanalysis, I don't know of a better one today but we know too much now about rationalization to be able to adopt it." Like so many of my generation who have been saved from many kinds of hypocrisy by the Freudian or Marxist premise that all thinking is "interested" thinking, I forgot that this rule applies just as much to denying as it does to affirming.

But here is Mr. Cammaerts who is clearly, in the best sense of that horrid word, a "normal" man. He does not hate his parents. He is a good husband and father. He likes people. He earns a steady living. Had he been brought up as a Christian and lived with people who went to church as a matter of course, it would have been natural that he should do the same, but why should he have felt so uneasy, so in need of an unconditional foundation? Lonely or ugly people, invalids, worldly failures, may need something more highly spiced, but for busy married citizens, surely humanism should be enough. Why should their nerve fail?

This, of course, is all nonsense. Our age has at least this advantage: its lack, except under extreme political pressure, of social, intellectual, or moral cohesion, the destruction by the machine of all natural and "closed" communities, its thoroughly urban character which exposes every individual to dozens of conflicting authorities and ideas, is making any merely traditional belief practically impossible. No doubt people will always be able to say "I believe" when they are really saying "We believe," to mistake for a personal act of affirmation what is only a passive submission to public opinion, but it is less easy to do this than it was, and the mass religions of our time, by their fanatical distrust of science and reason, their lack of continuity, their dependence on coercion and propaganda, betray themselves too clearly as fashions, as desperate attempts which are not even trusted by those who make them, *not* to be personally responsible for one's relation to truth.

We talk a great deal nowadays about the Common Man; actually there has never been an age which offered more to the exceptional man and less to the average. No longer hampered by a rigid social structure, his intellect no longer limited by traditional or provincial horizons, the gifted and the strong-willed have greater opportunities for good and evil than ever before. And is it not precisely among such people, whether scientists, artists, or businessmen, people who find their work fascinating and rewarded, that humanism, or government of the ego by the ego for the ego, is most easily accepted as a creed, for when one has great gifts, what answer to the meaning of existence should one require beyond the right to exercise them? Of what it must be like to be an average man whose work, particularly in an industrial society, can never content him or bring him fame, the gifted man has usually very little conception. Out of decency he may avoid the question of what such people, i.e. the majority of mankind, are to live by and for, by telling himself that a better organized society, a proper educational system, will make them as himself, but in his heart of hearts he knows that this is not so and that, humanistically speaking, there will always be an "elite" to which he is lucky enough to belong, and the "others," for whose existence there must, presumably, be a reason though he cannot imagine what it is, unless he concludes that they exist for his benefit, objects of compassion, maybe, to be looked after, fed, protected, amused, but objects nevertheless. Perhaps that is why the masses prefer the tyrant who quite frankly commands them to die for him to the goody-goody nursemaid who offers them sweets. The former is less insulting.

It has been said that the Church never recovered from the mass conversions of the Constantine age; if so, that problem is settled, for Christendom, the official Christendom attacked by Voltaire, Kierkegaard, Nietzsche and others, is already moribund. Even in Mr. Cammaerts' youth, one could be a freethinker without suffering any social or economic disadvantage, and within the last twenty years, even an active persecution of Christians has begun, and on the same charge as before, of political disloyalty. It is still possible, I fear, that in some countries an attempt will be made to "restore" the Christian religion as a political cement, to present the Word of God not as the good news but as a good thing to believe; such an attempt will fail—the contradiction between the Christian faith and the values of this world is too glaring

—but in so far as it is made, it will delay and not hasten the coming of the Kingdom.

Like falling in love, conversion is a decision which no one can be made to take, as he can be made to drive on the right-hand side of the road by the police, or made to see by logical necessity that two times two is four. The only persuasion that can influence a voluntary act is personal example. My own parents, for instance, were devout Christians who amazed and frightened me as a child by their sacrifice of themselves to my brothers and myself. I can remember wondering, while I took full advantage of their devotion: "How *can* they be so unselfish? I could never believe like that." I have thus been singularly fortunate in this respect, that I have always known that whether the Christian faith were true or false, the demands it made were so exacting that my self-love certainly hoped it were false.

Mr. Cammaerts rightly points out, however, that the example of personal conduct must include intellectual conduct, that is, dogma, the right thinking which is to a way of life as its grammar is to a language. For though, as Cardinal Newman said, we can no more argue a person into faith than one can torture him into it, a proper dogmatic instruction can at least prevent an intellectual from a very common rationalization of his will not to believe, which consists in inventing his own version of what Christians believe and then showing that that is intellectually or morally absurd. These imaginary versions, like their antidotes, are usually heresies. The materialist indentifies Christianity with Manichaeism, the aesthete with Arianism, the rationalist with belief in spooks and magical objects. Of course, individual Christians are guilty of all these just as they are of every other sin in the calendar, for it is just as difficult to be orthodox, i.e. not merely recite but fully assent to all the articles, as it is to be humble or chaste. One of the surest signs of a heresy is that it appeals to a certain kind of temperament or applies to a certain historical condition, and not at all to others. A heresy is an attempt to make God in one's own image; that is why there have to be so many different ones, to suit each person's idea of himself. The sanguine man finds the Incarnation easy to believe but is offended at the Cross; the choleric man is attracted by the heroism of the Cross, but repelled by the command to turn the other cheek; the melancholic man finds Original Sin an obvious truth, but the forgiveness of sins a difficult mystery.

But if he is to become a Christian, a man has to believe them all, for the Catholic faith, while it condemns no temperament as incapable of salvation, flatters none as being less in peril than any other. In the same way he has to make his public confession of belief in a church which is not confined to his sort, to those with whom by nature he feels at home, for in it there is neither Jew nor German, East nor West, boy nor girl, smart nor dumb, boss nor worker, Bohemian nor bourgeois, no elite of any kind; indeed there are not even Christians there, for Christianity is a way, not a state, and a Christian is never something one is, only something one can pray to become, aware always both of one's infinite capacity for rebellion and self-deception and of the infinite patience and love of God.

> From being anxious or secure,
> Dead clods of sadness or light squibs of mirth,
> From thinking that great courts immure
> All or no happiness, or that this earth
> Is only for our prison framed,
> Or that thou art covetous
> To them thou lovest, or that they are maimed
> From reaching this world's sweet who seek thee thus
> With all their might, Good Lord deliver us.

From needing danger to be good,
From owing thee yesterday's tears to-day,
    From trusting so much to thy blood
That in that hope we wound our soul away,
    From bribing thee with alms to excuse
    Some sin more burdenous,
From light affecting, in religion, news,
From thinking us all soul, neglecting thus
Our mutual duties, Lord deliver us.

W. H. AUDEN

Introduction

THE FAVOURABLE RECEPTION OF A RECENT BOOK[1] HAS encouraged me to gather together some notes written from time to time during these last two years.

I realize that my present attitude towards life and religion is shared by an increasing number of Christian writers of all denominations who are far better equipped than I am to express it in adequate terms.[2]

At the same time, I have noticed that unless general ideas are closely connected with personal experience many people have some difficulty in bringing them to bear on the social and historical conditions among which they live.

It is in order to smooth out these difficulties that I have once more exposed myself to the reproach of egotism by recording here the conclusions I have reached in the light of my somewhat varied experience.

It is hard for a man to confess that he has spent his life in search of truth, only to discover in his old age that he has wasted most of his energy in the pursuit of false illusions.

Nevertheless, if all writers of my generation who starting from atheism reached Christianity, recognized their past errors and proclaimed their new faith, their evidence might carry some weight to-day; and if all those who tried to find an aim in life through political systems and secular ideals admitted that none of these systems and ideals can bear fruit unless inspired by the spirit of God, the in-

---

[1] *Upon This Rock*, Harper & Brothers.
[2] *See* p. 176.

xix

fluence of Christianity might once more save the world from barbarism.

The journey from negation to faith coincides with the journey from Humanism to Christianity. I hope to show how I have come to think that most of the mistakes made by human society during the last four hundred years and the disastrous consequences which these mistakes have brought about, are due to the fact that man, instead of God, was placed in the centre of the universe. It is only when this tragic error is corrected that civilisation may emerge from the series of catastrophies in which it is at present involved.

My story is divided into seven chapters. Each of them is prefaced by a short autobiographical introduction, so that the reader may be acquainted with the circumstances which led me to my present opinions and beliefs.

I hope that I shall be forgiven for adopting a continental point of view, but the problems which I am considering concern not only Britain and America, but all western European countries. I also hope that the younger generation, which I have had especially in mind, will not grow impatient at what they might be inclined to call my pessimism. I have too much respect for the young men and women of to-day and too much sympathy for what they are going through, to try to attenuate or embellish the truth, as I see it.

EMILE CAMMAERTS

The Flower of Grass

I.

THE WORSHIP OF NATURE

I

I WAS BROUGHT UP, FROM MY EARLIEST YEARS, IN THE worship of nature. My mother's marriage had been a tragedy, a tragedy from which she never recovered. She had been granted a divorce, but my father had retained the custody of my two elder brothers. With no faith to support her, she had sought comfort, like many others of her generation, in the optimistic writings of Jean Jacques Rousseau. *Emile* was her bedside book. Following the "Master's" advice, she wished to stimulate my sense of wonder before the beauty of flowers and birds, fields and woods. During the long walks we took together in the surroundings of Brussels, which was not at that time the large straggling town which it is to-day, she taught me to recognize and appreciate natural objects and to respect them.

Having suffered from cruelty, she had developed an almost morbid hatred against any form of waste and suffering. I was told that plants and beasts were my friends, and strictly forbidden to inflict any pain upon them. I remember retracing my steps to pick up some flowers which I had inadvertently dropped on the way home. This led to a number of compromises because my natural possessiveness prompted me to collect a number of vegetable or animal "friends" which I met on the way. Plants were carefully uprooted, placed in a tin box, and planted in our garden. If flowers were gathered, vases had to be

1

found for them, so that their lives should be prolonged. I had to give up the idea of transfixing beetles in glass frames, but an exception was made in the case of moths and butterflies, on condition that they were "put to sleep."

Since I had little opportunity of observing the open country—my usual playground being a large park in the immediate neighbourhood—my mother succeeded in eliminating from my mind any idea that nature was ruthless. This character was reserved not to man, but to certain men. She did not however succeed in hiding from me some manifestations of ruthlessness and cruelty which fascinated me all the more because they did not tally with her teaching. The best tended park has its rival ant-heaps, the most secluded garden has its spiders' webs, the most comfortable house may be infected with mice with which a cat may be seen to play with delightful skill. I was too young to realize the contradictions between such observations and the law of goodness impressed upon me, but I was not too young to be sincerely disturbed by them.

The seed sown by my loving mother germinated in my adolescence when for the first time I had an opportunity of exploring the hills and forests of the Ardennes. If I had entertained any doubt about the essential goodness of nature, they were dispelled by the joy I felt in this discovery. It was a vague feeling no doubt, in which the pleasure of physical exercise, the spirit of adventure and the contemplation of a picturesque and varied landscape, were strongly confused. I was unable to discriminate between the pleasant effect which these excursions had upon me and the fundamental character of the new surroundings in which I was placed. Because I derived from them a peace of mind and a physical satisfaction which I had never experienced before, I concluded that they possessed moral qualities. Deprived of all religious teaching and groping unconsciously towards some concrete ideal which might fill my soul and bring some relief from the tension from which I suffered in a sharply divided family, I believed that I had at last discovered a safe refuge from the doubts which had oppressed my early childhood. I began to consider nature as a person, as a fruitful and generous spirit which would help me on my way and give me the support and comfort I sorely needed.

I remember particularly a steep hill which I had made a point of "climbing" on my bicycle while my companions dismounted one after the other. Waiting for them at the top, I sat on a rock and looked down a narrow valley covered with birches and larches which broadened towards the winding river and the small town we had left behind. It was an early morning in June. The ground sparkled in the sun and the dew was lifting in long trailing scarves from the valley. The air was filled with the clamour of birds, and such a feeling of peace came over me that I felt relieved of all anxieties, about my mother who was ill at the time and from whom I was separated, about the wickedness of those who inflicted suffering upon her, about my own future if anything happened to her. "Surely," I said to myself, "nothing can be wrong in such a beautiful world."

There is nothing exceptional in this experience. A boy brought up in a Christian family might have expressed himself somewhat differently by saying: "This is God's creation. If I cannot grasp the mysteries of religion, I can at least understand this 'beautiful world.' If I needed a concrete proof of the goodness of God, I should find it here." The same illusion would have provoked the same error.

. . . . .

This error is caused by the confusion between the impression of comfort or beauty and the virtue of goodness.

Personal exaltation becomes a guarantee of moral excellence. Because the contemplation of a particular landscape did me good, I concluded that nature as such was good. Self-centredness is not confined to the agnostic, but it is increased by agnosticism or by a weak religion. To worship nature after two thousand years of Christianity is sheer nonsense; to worship God in nature is a dangerous heresy. This nonsense or heresy permeated all the works of art, all the poetry and a great deal of the music which I most admired at the time, and I found in their true beauty some support for the false ideas which my personal experience had given me of the natural world.

In my school days, I read Lamartine and Alfred de Musset, and listened to the rich descriptive music produced in the nineteenth century, from Beethoven's *Pastoral Symphony* to Wagner's *Walweben*. Later, when I haunted art galleries and exhibitions, I was most attracted by landscape painting. The mission of art, music and literature seemed to me to glorify the spirit of nature through words, sounds and colours. I found in these works a confirmation of my own belief that trees and beasts were far more interesting than men. I was at home in a forest. There I found myself among faithful friends. Woods and hills, rivers and fields, gave me a strange impression of security. They had been there before I was born and would be there after my death. I knew when I left them that I could find them again, that they would always be ready to welcome me and relieve my loneliness. Because I loved them for their smiling beauty I fondly imagined that they loved me. I never missed a Sunday walk and thought that I found in a wood a stronger inspiration than that which I could find in a church. The music of birds and waving branches was better than any organ, and the smell of dead leaves and pines scorched by the sun better than incense. The trunks of beeches and the high vault of their branches were the columns and arches of my cathedral. This unconscious pantheism filled me with a wild enthusiasm. I felt at one with "Mother Nature." It was for me that she filled the sky with the glow of sunset, and shook the earth with her thunder. For me, the stars sparkled in the darkness and the night flooded the world with the dream of moonshine. When this ecstasy brought tears to my eyes, the wind which dried them was Nature's own breath.

Most sensitive boys pass through such a phase, especially when their religious instinct has been thwarted by a strictly secular education. The joy which I derived from nature worship was no doubt rendered more acute by an extreme shyness which paralysed me when I had any opportunity of meeting a girl of my own age. These opportunities were besides very rare because I obstinately refused to comply with the conventions which permeated the society in which I lived. To pay a call on people who were not my friends seemed to me sheer hypocrisy, and since I never accepted a formal invitation I soon lost the opportunity of doing so. Sexual repression combined with religious repression to strengthen my belief that wild and free nature should be the centre of man's universe and that with her alone he could enter into true communion.

This belief was shared by my elder brother who had been allowed to join us when he entered university. We differed in everything else, in politics, tastes and manners, but agreed wholeheartedly on this all-important issue. In his quiet way he was perhaps more closely absorbed in nature than I was. Being of a more retiring disposition he disapproved of the ardent friendships in which I soon indulged among my fellow students. I had enjoyed home life as a boy; he had been deprived of it. I was imaginative, prompt to sudden enthusiasm; he was, to all appearances, cool and sensible. I neglected my most essential duties to help strangers; he was scrupulously attentive in fulfilling his responsibilities, but did not like to venture outside the family circle. How his prudence joined my recklessness is a mystery which only his tolerance for the younger brother he wished to protect from the world can possibly explain. Anyhow, nature was our bond. We tramped together on every occasion, in every season, and our excursions extended from the Ardennes to the Rhineland and from the Rhineland to the Alps. We made walking a fine art, and became practically independent of the round of inns and hotels which cramp the style of tourists. We went to see what we wished to see, and if we found no other accommodation, slept in the heather or under the shelter of trees.

I learned to respect my brother's silence. We seldom interrupted the rhythm of our steps. When we did, it was for a scanty meal in a well-chosen place or, in summer, for a rest during the heat of the day. We travelled light and found a perverse pleasure in the discomforts of rough living. To "fast" on bread and cheese, to be lashed by wind and rain was a kind of self-mortification: the price we had to pay.

We never allowed the weather to interfere with our plans and discovered a way of resting even when the ground was covered with mud or snow by leaning on each other's backs, for a long space of time. On these occasions, our voices were hushed by the mystery of the woods, and we listened to the patter of the rain and the strange noise of the wind in the trees, like the shouting of a distant crowd. Our attention was divided between the map and the landscape. It would have been impossible for us to discriminate between the satisfaction we derived from physical exercise and the joy we found in colours, shapes and sounds. Our itinerary was so carefully prepared that we were seldom disturbed by a discordant noise or any sign of modern industry. Civilisation had driven us from the roads; we followed devious footpaths or made our way across the country. We prided ourselves on walking thirty miles without meeting an "ugly sight" and made a point of never returning to a favourite spot which had been spoiled by man's "vandalism."

. . . . .

I should be ungrateful if I did not acknowledge these joys, but my gratefulness goes now to God who gave me eyes to see the beauty of the world, and made me able to perceive that in man and nature there are certain common features which can be recognized as the stamp of God's creation. I am not grateful to an unconscious divinity which did nothing to justify my worship or to answer my love. Nature is no longer the goal, but with love, friendship, social intercourse, one of the many means of reaching the goal.

I had already drawn this conclusion when I met my brother for the last time in a sanatorium in Switzerland, a few weeks before the outbreak of the war. We discussed the political situation, whether this new crisis would blow over like the last, whether Switzerland would be invaded, whether Belgium would once more be the victim of aggression, and when and how it would be possible for him to join his family in Brussels before the storm broke out. I still see him, on my last visit, feeding the birds which hopped on the window-sill. "Whatever happens," he said, "don't worry about me. I am not alone." And, pointing to the great snow-clad peaks on the opposite side of the Rhône valley, he added: "I walk through the mountains every day without leaving my bed. I shall never be tired of the sight of them."

He knows now that there was a great deal of misanthropy in our worship, and that nature was for us merely a means of escaping from an unfriendly world. We lent it virtues which it did not possess, because it did not show so evidently as human society the evil forces which warp the whole creation. Those very mountains through which my brother walked in imagination during his last days were indifferent to his slow agony. They glowed in the sunset one day and, the next day, would drop their avalanches upon the villages nestling at their feet. My brother knows now better than I do that the world of men, in spite of its meanness and ugliness, is infinitely more important than the natural scenery which surrounds it. He knows the vanity of the illusions which sustained our steps when we tramped together, shoulder to shoulder, over our favourite hills. He has reached the end of his journey, and the power to believe which he sought so eagerly and sincerely in this world has at last been given him.

II

Most men are not inclined to worship nature or to give it human qualities and feelings. Town dwellers usually consider the open country as a playing field where they can enjoy the healthy relaxation of games and sports. Hills and woods are a fitting frame for racing and hunting, or, to use the modern word, for hiking. If we add a casual interest in flowers and birds and a natural greed for fruit, this is the average reaction provoked by nature on most people to-day.

This was also the attitude of all classes, including the aristocracy, during fifteen centuries of Christian civilisation. Apart from those pastorals which record the frolics of the peasantry, and a few descriptive touches in epics and romances, the feeling for nature is rarely expressed in mediaeval literature. The number of birds referred to, if we except the lark and the nightingale, is extremely restricted. Flowers are seldom singled out. In art, hills and trees are roughly indicated, merely to show that the scene is set in a "desert" or uninhabited place. Trees are drawn like glorified cabbages and hills like lumps of carved cheese, even in Giotto's finest frescoes. It was not until the fifteenth century that any effort was made to reproduce natural objects with care or accuracy.

This neglect of the wilder aspects of the landscape by poets and artists corresponded to the instinctive hostility of the country folk towards the woods which surrounded their farms and the hills which enclosed their valleys. These woods and hills were the haunt of robbers and wild beasts, such as wolves and bears. They had been the refuge of criminals and the scene of their crimes since the days of the "Babes in the Wood" and "Hansel and Gretel," the place where sorcerers and magicians prepared their plots in the dark. Even to-day the farmer retains an inveterate prejudice against trees which throw their shadow over his crops, and mountains which make ploughing harder and fill the soil with stones.

We often meet in mediaeval art and literature tame beasts, like the dog, the horse and the cow, which had become part of human life. We also meet a number of semi-fantastic animals, an inheritance from Greek or Asiatic folklore. The *"bestiaires"* speak of pelicans and unicorns, of the phoenix rising from its ashes and satanic dragons and griffins. These were portrayed again and again, not for their intrinsic interest, but for their symbolic meaning, like the mystic rose and the virginal lily. The same use was made of the sun, the moon, the stars and the signs of the zodiac, corresponding to every month of the year and to its traditional occupation. Every natural object was looked upon, not for itself, but as connected with God or man. It was a word in the dictionary of the Christian language.

Nature was, no doubt, considered as part of the creation but it stood outside human preoccupations which were centred on the relationship between man and God. The earth had been given to man to be used by him. The fields were there to be ploughed, the corn to be reaped, the horse to be trained and harnessed, the pig to be fattened and killed, the fruit to be gathered, the fish to be caught, and the wild beasts and fowls to be hunted. The feeling for nature, as it remains to-day in the countryside, was mostly a feeling of proprietorship. It would have seemed as ridiculous to worship nature as to worship a cart or a table. It would have seemed as ridiculous to squander the gifts of nature or to disfigure them as to squander an heirloom.

In short, man placed nature in the scheme of things exactly where it should be placed. It was a possession to be administered carefully and wisely, without sentimentality or wasteful cruelty. It is curious to notice that it is precisely when the fashion for nature worship begins that such waste and cruelty manifest themselves in their crudest forms. The rise of Romanticism coincides with the industrial revolution.

For the modern peasant, as for the mediaevalist, nature does not possess any moral quality. It is not, like man, the battlefield of good and evil, it is neither good nor evil. It is neither an example to be followed, nor a temptation to be avoided. It is, as most parables of the Gospel show, the source from which the shepherd, the vine-grower and the fisherman draw their living. It exists on a lower plane than man who, in his turn, dwells on a lower plane than God.

Mediaeval art, in the carvings of the cathedrals, the frescoes covering the walls of the churches and in illuminated manuscripts, reflects this hierarchy of importance and interest. God and His angels come first, the Virgin and the Saints come next, while man and his work in the field and the workshop take third rank. Nature only appears in so far as it is connected with man's labours. It lies at the bottom of the scale.[1]

. . . . .

It may be useful to meet here an objection which has no doubt crossed the reader's mind. Did not man, from the beginning of civilisation, consider certain natural aspects and objects as good or propitious, and others as bad or unpropitious? Was not a distinction made between light and darkness, the day and the night, the daisy and the nettle, the lamb and the lion, the dog and the wolf, the dove and the serpent, the bee and the wasp?

This distinction has two origins which are both associated with man's life and with his reaction to his surroundings.

The first depends on man's material interest. Some beasts and some plants happen to be useful and are liked for their usefulness, other beasts and other plants happen to be useless or harmful and are disliked accordingly. A natural phenomenon may be "bad" in certain circumstances and "good" in others. Rain may be blessed in the summer or in a hot climate, and cursed in the autumn or in a wet climate. A storm is beneficent when it breaks a spell of drought and malevolent when it devastates the crops.

[1] The verses of the Sermon on the Mount, in which we are told to "behold the fowls of the air," and to "consider the lilies of the field," have often been misinterpreted.

Christ does not suggest that nature should serve as a model to man; He simply uses it as an illustration for His reasoning: "If God so clothe the grass of the field which to-day is, and to-morrow is cast into the oven, shall He not *much more* clothe you, O ye of little faith?"

The second origin is rooted in man's sensibility, although frequently connected with his interest. It is difficult to decide whether the impression of evil we have when faced with a serpent, is derived from the fact that certain snakes are poisonous or from the leglessness of the animal. Apart from the element of interest which is obvious in this case, our impression may be the result of human imagination expressed in legends and fables. It does not rest on any sure foundation and cannot justify any moral judgment.

. . . . . .

Whether the amoral character of nature is due to original sin, which disrupted at the same time the relationship between man and God and between the human creature and the rest of the creation, or whether the fall of man released some wild chaotic force which must be tamed or subdued before order is restored, the fact remains that the character of disorder is as evident in nature as the character of sin is in man. It is no doubt wrong to say that human history is entirely ruled by economic laws which ensure the survival of the fittest and the elimination of the weak. But it is not wrong to say that, if nature is not interfered with by man, it is dominated by the struggle for existence. In the jungle, or the desert, every beast preys on every other beast, every plant, every tree lives at the expense of another plant or another tree which is either stunted or stifled. The tenderest bird feeds on insects and grubs; even the lamb grazes on daisies and buttercups. Appearances are deceptive.

The laws of nature constantly referred to by modern authors, should not be compared with human law. They are mainly useful generalisations, showing that, in the light of human reason, certain phenomena bring about certain results. They are not concerned with our religious or moral development. Human law, on the contrary, has, from the origin of civilisation, been based on some religious principle. It is the expression of commandments given to men by some supernatural being. It was because this being was supernatural that the commandments were first accepted and were embodied in a code of law. Being man-made, this adaptation of the divine law to human conditions is necessarily imperfect. "Thou shalt not steal" covers all kinds of robbery, while the laws enforced by society leave many loopholes and often allow the great criminals to escape while the petty criminals are caught and punished. However, the tendency of civilisation to introduce some kind of order into an orderless world is evident. Under the influence of religion, man has transformed plunder into property, sexual promiscuity into marriage, arbitrary tyranny into legal authority. The law of Rome prepared the way for Christianity, and one of the main preoccupations of the Church in the Dark Ages was to restore the social order which had been broken by the Barbarians. The obedience to secular power mentioned in the Gospels and emphasized in the Pauline epistles, is not so much in contrast to the rest of the New Testament teaching as would at first appear. God has never acted through anarchy.

I am writing these lines sitting on a hill overlooking a wide valley in the Cotswolds, while some aeroplanes circle above my head engaged in flying practice. The landscape, with its small woods, cultivated fields and peaceful villages, is gentle enough. The air is so still that the clouds seem to be fixed for ever in the sky, and the slender column of smoke rising from the chimney of a farm nearby looks as if it had been painted on the background of the dark beeches. Here the cruelty of nature is well hidden, and if I allowed my imagination to get the better of my common sense I might reflect, as I would have reflected twenty years ago, on the pathetic contrast between this piece of land bathed in the powdered light of a fine evening, and the horror and tumult of war suggested by the circling planes and the rattle of their machine guns.

But the battle for life, the triumph of the strong and the defeat of the weak, are here as they are on the battlefield. On the very bank on which I am sitting, hundreds of insects are slipping between the blades of grass like ravenous beasts in a virgin forest, flying, pursuing, falling into spiders' webs, snapped up by a hungry bird, killing or being killed. A lark rises, a few yards away, ready to start "its magic trill," but it hovers for one moment, interrupting its song, and drops like a hawk on its prey. The fighting is pursued everywhere. Its results may be very slow. The stifling of the pine tree which I see on the fringe of that wood, by the ivy clinging closely round its trunk, may take many years, but it is not less deadly for that. The circling planes do not create a contrast; they complete the picture. They show what happens when the struggle of beast against beast and plant against plant becomes the struggle of man against man.

Some Romantics refused to recognize this conflict; others, like Tennyson, found serious difficulty in reconciling it to their preconceived idea of the fundamental goodness of nature and man.

> Who trusted God was love indeed
> And love Creation's final law—
> Tho' Nature, red in tooth and claw
> With ravine, shriek'd against his creed.[2]

While the state of open warfare has hitherto been merely an interruption in man's life, it has always been the rule in nature's life. Nature is non-religious, amoral and—in the true sense of the word—lawless. Animals have no treaty to respect, no honour to preserve, no faith to keep. That is why one of the most horrible pictures human imagination can conjure up is a beast turned into a man

[2] "In Memoriam," LVI.

(like the ambiguous beings of H. G. Wells' *The Island of Doctor Moreau,* or beasts acting as men, like the insects in Capek's play. The fact that the herd instinct may substitute the lawlessness of the pack to the lawlessness of the individual does not affect this conclusion. A man who makes a beast of himself is not only objectionable or a disgusting man, he is a man who is on the way to losing his soul, and to severing all connection with God or any ideal which he has substituted for God. He is a man on the threshold of Hell.

We say that beasts "don't know any better," but man does know better, and when he turns into a beast, he becomes far worse than a beast. That is what the mediaeval artists tried to express when they gave the devil horns, a tail and a hoof. Satan is as different from the "Great god Pan" as his demons are from the satyrs who danced through the woods of Greece. These were personifications of natural forces, like most pagan gods. They suggest nature's effort to rise to the level of man. Demons are spirits debased below the level of nature.

Jérôme Bosch and Breughel, in the sixteenth century, preserved this sound tradition when they gave their devils a form in which animal shapes, such as fish, crabs or insects, are combined with human shapes. In his "Fight of the Fallen Angels," Breughel opposes the angelic form— a human being flying on wings, risen from earthly to heavenly status—to demoniac forms, such as a combination of woman, moth and turnip—a human being degraded to the status of an insect or a vegetable. This touch of grim humour had completely disappeared by the time Milton wrote his *Paradise Lost,* in which he sometimes represents even Satan as beautiful.

> He above the rest
> In shape and gesture proudly eminent
> Stood like a Tower; his form had yet not lost

All her original brightness, nor appear'd
Less than Arch Angel ruin'd, and th' excess
Of Glory obscur'd.

. . . . . .

How were man's ideas so deeply altered that he turned the world upside down and substituted the worship of nature to the worship of God?

The process of transformation from the sixteenth to the eighteenth century was so gradual that it was scarcely noticed at the time. It developed side by side with the rise of Humanism which placed man, instead of God, in the centre of the universe.

We are sufficiently separated from that period of time to realize that the one could not have taken place without the other, that the assumed hegemony of man must lead to the assumed hegemony of nature.

Some of the philosophers who paved the way for the French Revolution did not wish to challenge the principles of divine authority. Rousseau involved himself in strange contradictions in order to avoid this danger. But, contemporary with Rousseau were Voltaire, Diderot and the encyclopedists who were keenly opposed not only to the Church but to the idea of any supernatural influence. Their followers did not hesitate to challenge all authority, human and divine, except their own. The commandments of God being ignored, law ceased to be looked upon as inspired by God. It was made by man for his own use and could be altered by him. It gradually lost its moral and permanent value. It became merely the expression of the will of the regime prevailing at the time.

The supernatural plane of the universe having been removed, man found himself obliged to search elsewhere for a justification for his actions. A vague theism still survived, a reverence for "Providence," the "Creator," the

"Architect of the Universe." God was no longer Judge or Redeemer. He was merely responsible for nature; and man, unable to look for Him in Heaven and still disturbed by an obscure religious instinct, began to look for Him on earth.

This trend of thought coincided with the development of "sensibility" among the intellectuals. Sensibility was the result of a reaction against rationalism, on the one side, and against social conventions, on the other. It idealized everything which stimulated the imagination or played on sentiment, and proclaimed the freedom of love. Rousseau is the author of the *"Contrat Social"* which illustrates the political aspect of the movement, and of *"La Nouvelle Héloise"* which illustrates its sentimental aspect. He is also the author of the *"Rêveries d'un promeneur solitaire"* which reveals its attitude towards nature.

Rousseau and Bernardin de St. Pierre, like Coleridge and Wordsworth in their youth, and most of the romantics who followed them, revelled in solitude, not the intimacy of their study, but the solitude of woods and hills. These humanitarians never seem so happy as when they succeed in escaping from the company of man. Nature is both their teacher and their comforter. She—I use the personal pronoun intentionally because for them nature is a person— she comforts them in their trouble, because she gives them peace and does not "intrude upon their meditations"; she tells them that man should live, unhampered in his desires, sincere and innocent, freed from all conventions, allowing life and love to exercise their irresistible power. Nature is "God's incarnation," she reflects His image. The thinker or the poet loses himself in his contemplation, his being is absorbed by the light of the setting sun and the rising moon, by the song of birds, by the rustling of the trees in the wind, by the scent of flowers, by the rhythmic lapping of the waves against the shore. The scene is generally a lake, because a tranquil sheet of water reflecting the trees and rocks enhances the mystic influence of the new divinity.

Rousseau wishes to "lose himself, to annihilate himself, in Nature as in some beloved being." For Wordsworth, she is "the breath of God." For Coleridge her "shape and sounds" are the words.

> Of that eternal language which thy God
> Utters, who from eternity doth teach
> Himself in all, and all things in Himself.

And Lamartine exclaims:

> *Mais la Nature est là qui t'invite et qui t'aime,*
> *Plonge toi dans son sein qu'elle t'ouvre toujours*
> *Dieu, pour le concevoir a fait l'intelligence:*
> *Sous la nature enfin découvre son auteur!*
> *Une voix à l'esprit parle dans son silence:*
> *Qui n'a pas entendu cette voix dans son coeur?*

Such is the wonder and the illusion from which we have scarcely recovered.

. . . . . .

It was a true wonder because the poetry founded on this error remains one of the finest expressions of the human soul. Nature, already discovered by the Elizabethans and by the poets of the French *"Pléiade"* as the frame of human life, the scenery of the human drama, was rediscovered as the reflection of the vague divinity which had been substituted for God. In her, man found his joy and inspiration, his pain and tragedies, enlarged and glorified. He no longer felt himself to be puny and weak, oppressed by adversity, but a semi-god roving through the world with the "West Wind," the "Cloud," the storm or the cataract. He rose to heaven, not on angels' but on eagles' wings, he reigned in majesty like "Mont Blanc." The flowers were his thoughts, and the light which flooded the sunset shone through his own soul. Like Turner, he pictured himself in nature. He identified himself with her and, since she was the image of a dethroned God, he felt exalted by the vision of his own divinity. The strength and enthusiasm which this heresy aroused gave birth to a number of wonderful works, and the legitimate pride which the poet and his admirers felt in them confirmed their belief that they were founded on truth.

> Beauty is truth, truth beauty—that is all
> Ye know on earth, and all ye need to know.

Struck by the beauty of a wild landscape, the Romantic imagines that it must be both morally good and true. He has, like any other man, a desire for unity and wishes to bring together the things which he most admires and respects. In the Middle Ages this could be done without confusion, for every admirable object was of God, and everything detestable was touched by the evil spirit. But in the nineteenth century the authority of God was no longer recognized and the devil was not even mentioned. The "Architect of the Universe" was responsible for the whole edifice of creation, from its loftiest turrets to its darkest cellars. It is on this pathetic attempt at harmony that the worship of nature was based.

Not only had the modern humanist singled out all the pleasant phenomena in nature and thrown a veil over the unpleasant, changing the proportions of the picture, but he had explained these pleasant facts by the supposed intervention of an all-wise providence. The Architect had made the flowers bright in order to attract the insects which collect the honey and pollinate the stamens. Had He also made the ephemeral flies bright in order that the fish should catch them more easily? He had given caterpillars the colour of the plants on which they fed, so that they should escape their enemies. Did this arrangement suit the plant? The only God which the humanists of the period recognized was as capricious and inconsistent as the world which was supposed to reflect his purpose.[3]

Confusion became worse confounded because the Romantics did not distinguish between scientific and moral truth, or between natural and artistic beauty.

In the scientific sense, nature is true because, if accurately observed, the facts of nature correspond to man's perception of them. But in the moral sense, nature cannot be true because, being deprived of consciousness, she does not possess any notion of responsibility.[4]

To the poet, nature is beautiful because, being like man part of the creation, her shapes and colours, her sounds and scents awake in him a feeling of wonder akin to recognition. He might say that even the most grotesque animals, such as the camel and the hippopotamus, or the most terrifying, such as the spider and the octopus, are admirable and even beautiful. But they are not beautiful in the same sense as a work of art is beautiful.

When we appreciate a work of art we admire the achievement of a particularly gifted man who succeeds in translating into words, shapes, colours or sounds, some impressions he has received from his surroundings. The quality of this achievement depends on the quality of the translation. What we admire in the "Castle of Steen" or in the "Haywain" is not the natural landscape, but the representation of that natural landscape by Rubens or Constable on a piece of canvas, with the help of a brush and a few colours. The wonder we experience does not come from nature, but from man. A masterpiece is a piece of

---

[3] This teleological argument is used both by the Catholic Chateaubriand, as a proof of the existence of God, and by the free-thinker Michelet, as a proof of the harmony of the Universe.

[4] I am not dealing with the supposed "conscience" of domestic pets.

nature integrated by the genius of the master, raised from the unconscious to the conscious state.

.   .   .   .   .   .

Since he refused to recognize sin in man the romantic humanist refused also to recognize the effect of sin upon nature. He therefore established an artificial connection between the fundamental goodness of man—unspoilt by civilisation—and the complete truth, goodness and beauty of nature—unmarred by the defects of human society.

The pagan method was better, because the illusion it created proceeded according to the natural hierarchy which places man above nature. There is a true joy running through some Greek myths and their animation of natural forces. Something of this boisterous exaltation of the "good things of life" persists in the Renaissance, in Venetian art, in Elizabethan poetry, and even in some aspects of the baroque period, such as Rubens' glowing pageantry. Harmony is preserved between the blindness of nature and the mad irresponsibility of the satyrs and nymphs of the bacchanals. But the Romantic denied this irresponsibility. They pursued their illusions, while preserving their moral consciousness, and since nature did not possess and could not give them what they hoped to find in her, their illusions were followed by disillusionment.

The reason given by the Romantic for his love of solitude was that, when he was alone with nature, he felt nearer to God, since nature was a perfect image of God, whereas God's work had been spoilt in man by "civilisation." How this civilisation, being of human origin, could have altered the original perfection of man without the interference of sin is never explained.

To make "civilisation" responsible for human sufferings

is to forget that the same developments in technique and social relations which have been so much misused in modern days, have to a great extent emancipated man from the misery and terror of "natural life" and given him a sense of security in a hostile world. In human as in natural things, we discover two conflicting tendencies, the only difference is that nature, being unconscious, has no "knowledge" of guilt. This is no reason for raising its unconscious "innocence" to the level of a real innocence, and its too evident brutality to the level of a less evident virtue.

A man who is "wrapt" in himself is inclined to worship nature because he worships himself in nature. A man keenly interested in other men and women is not likely to pay so much attention to his natural surroundings. He is at home in a house, in a city, in a church. His keenest wish is not to rove about the world, to scale the Alps or to challenge the stormy seas. He need not seek God in glaciers and cataracts.

There is a strange perversion in this worship of the lower stages of life; there is also a strain of weakness. We often seek the comfort of nature after a disappointment in our social life, because we lack the courage to persevere. As men, it is our social life which is our natural battleground. We are not born hermits, we are born into a family, among citizens, and it is our relationship with the members of our family and our neighbours which is the keystone of our life.

Christians believe that such a relationship can be neither friendly nor fruitful if it is not governed by laws which are inspired by the revelation of God. They estimate the value of their interests in the light of this revelation. They do not despise nature, they love it as that unconscious part of creation through which God manifests Himself. They both respect and love other men because they are the conscious creation of the same God. But they worship God alone because He is the source of all unconscious and conscious power and goodness, the one Authority in whose Love they, as men, are free to act.

I was shown recently, in a museum, a shapeless block of wood riddled with nails. I learnt that this block represented a god made by some natives of the South Sea Islands, into which they had driven nails in order to make sure that their prayers should be heard. The idol was unperturbed by this rough treatment. The nature worship of the Romantics is very akin to this primitive practice. They do not make the tree a god in human shape and endowed with human passions, as the pagans did, neither do they consider it as a humble unconscious part of God's creation, as the Christians do. They worship the tree as a god made of wood and fling their arms around its trunk in a desperate attempt to "merge themselves" into the silent rising of the sap.[5]

The so-called progress of godless man may be represented by a serpent biting its own tail. The last developments of modern sensibility have brought us back to the first crude expression of the religious instinct. There is however another tree of which a Cross was made. And the nails were not only driven through the wood of the Cross but through the hands and feet of God, crucified on that Cross.

[5] In *L'Arbre*, Emile Verhaeren describes how he feels the tree's life reach his own heart:

> *"Et j'appuyais sur lui ma poitrine brutale,*
> *Avec un tel amour, une telle ferveur,*
> *Que son rythme profound et sa force totale*
> *Passaient en moi et pénétraient jusqu'à mon coeur."*

The conclusion is inevitable: "Strength is holy."

II.

TRUTH, BEAUTY AND GOODNESS

I

ONE OF THE GRAVEST MISTAKES WHICH CHRISTIANS MADE, IN the last century, was to denounce secularism as immoral. I never met a more strictly moral person than my mother. Truth was the foundation of her very life. I have forgotten the subject of the quarrel she had with one of our oldest friends, but the scene left a strong impression on me because the lady burst into tears before leaving the house; I was fond of her and I realized that I should never see her again.

My grandmother, who was of a far more tolerant disposition and who had tried in vain to pour oil on troubled waters, remarked, shaking her head: "There goes another friend who has become our enemy."

"I don't care for any friendship," retorted my mother, "which is based on a lie."

"It is always better to tell the truth," said my grandmother, "but it is not always necessary to tell the whole truth."

This dialogue characterizes the attitude of the two women with whom I spent my youth, and I need scarcely add that I instinctively sided with my mother.

We had, she explained to me, a mysterious thing called conscience which had to be scrupulously respected. If we did our duty, and kept all our promises, our conscience would be clear, and our first duty was to tell the truth, without any regard for the consequences. She made me

24

look into a mirror. She blew upon it and I saw that the reflection of my face was blurred. Then she wiped it with her handkerchief and showed me how it became bright again: "That is what happens to you when you tell a lie, and this when you tell me that you have told a lie."

I tried in vain to believe in this conscience, but I only succeeded in believing more and more in my mother. Because her tenderness was what I valued most in the world and because it seemed to freeze into a hard indifference whenever I broke her rules, I did my best to obey them. This task was rendered more easy by the fact that the orders I received were not arbitrary and that I realized how much my interest was considered. Nevertheless, the efforts I made to "be good" depended mostly on my deep-rooted attachment to the person on whom my security and happiness were founded. When I failed to understand or pretended not to understand her instructions, my mother used her supreme argument: "Do it to please me," which later became: "If you don't do it, you don't love me." My spiritual life was based on this personal appeal.

.   .   .   .   .

What was wrong with the moral teaching I received before I entered a secondary school was not its looseness, but rather its strictness. Secular morality, at that time, took the form of self-righteousness. An almost puritanical worship of truth and goodness was substituted for the worship of God. It was a self-centred faith from which all sense of humour had disappeared. People who have decided to direct their own destiny are bound to take themselves too seriously.

The few friends I met in my mother's house were honest and good, according to their lights, but these lights were dimmed by rationalism and lack of charity. Many nineteenth century bourgeois were most conscientious. They cultivated their conscience as a gardener might cultivate a sunless garden. If it produced few flowers, it was not because it was not properly tended, but because some plants stifled the others and because the sun of God did not shine upon them. The free-thinkers had no master to show them the relation of honesty to love. They were left to their own devices and, just as certain sects worship the "God within," they worshipped the "conscience within" and thought themselves justified in acting as judges in their own case. They were not in revolt against the law; on the contrary, they obeyed it to the letter; but they were in revolt against the spirit which is the true law. The nineteenth century bourgeois was not immoral, he was so moral that morality—*i.e.*, observance of a certain standard of decency—had become his religion. He was, to all intents and purposes, a secular Pharisee.

Because I was often ill in those days, I was given private lessons by a young master from a neighbouring preparatory school. M. Hulin did his best to impress upon me a sense of duty and tried to show me the difference between right and wrong. It was right to obey my mother because I would hurt her if I did not do so, and "did I wish to hurt my dear mother?" It was right to perform the tasks he set me to do, and he would be disappointed if I did not perform them, and "did I wish to disappoint him?" I was assured that to tell a lie, to be selfish or violent was "unworthy of me." This gave me, beside an exaggerated opinion of my own importance, the feeling that I could win M. Hulin's esteem and affection by behaving according to plan. As he was infinitely patient, I had no difficulty in doing this, and soon basked in the sun of his indulgence. I still entertained a healthy fear of my mother's perspicacity, but had no scruple in using and abusing M. Hulin's gentleness. This new personal appeal was more easy to answer than the first. It was also far more dangerous, because my young master's prestige was not destined to last very long.

Atheists imagine that they can do away with religion and that it is enough to deny God to suppress spiritual activity. In fact, there is no such thing as complete atheism. Diverted from its natural channel by anti-Christian prejudice, spiritual activity will follow some other channel. The society among which I moved was dominated by the ideal of Freedom, but since the un-hampered exercise of freedom proved impracticable, it had been fenced within limits called Conscience, Truth, Right and Justice. Goodness had become the handmaid of self-righteousness, and Beauty was supposed to crown the edifice.

As far as I can remember, I remained indifferent to this abstract system and to these vague loyalties. My God, therefore, became my Mother, and his attendants, a small number of persons, like M. Hulin, to whom I was particularly devoted. This Mother-God and her saints embodied all the good things of the world and it was enough to love them and to be loved by them to feel relatively secure. The idea that I might lose my mother haunted my dreams, and I made her promise that she would never die as long as I lived. This must have seriously strained her sense of truthfulness.

When I reached the age of adolescence my faith in her infallible wisdom began to be shaken, and I realized that the saints I worshipped were not essentially different from other men and women, and were like them apt to make mistakes. I could find nowhere that image of absolute perfection which I so much needed.

.   .   .   .   .

The position of a boy who leaves the shelter of home to enter a school is always difficult. It is likely to be more difficult if this experience is delayed by ill-health, and it is bound to become dangerous if he has been brought up outside the Church.

I had not been baptized; I had never read the Gospel. Although everything was done to hide from me the "ugly side of life," I was not ignorant of the fact that there might be evil forces at work in the world. Such demons, however, remained in the background; they did not belong to everyday reality. The very terror which they inspired made them strange and remote. Everything I had been taught led me to believe that evil was the exception, and goodness the rule. Rousseau, "Jean-Jacques" as my mother familiarly called him, declared that if man was not good it was not his fault, and that children, being closer to nature, retained their natural innocence.

The school to which I was sent was not worse than any other. It was a typical State secular school, where five hundred boys, who came from all kinds of homes, struggled through the curriculum under the control of efficient masters. Judged by English standards, the instruction was good, but education was sorely neglected. What filled me with amazement was the cynicism with which the boys broke all the rules I had been told to respect. Their only moral principle seemed to be not to tell on one another. For the rest, every lie, every trick was allowed and even admired if it succeeded. To be found out seemed the only crime, to be clever and "in the know," the only virtue, and "the know" included a string of obscene words and practices which filled me with a horror not unmixed with secret temptations. This caused the first breach in my intimacy with my mother. After placing her on such a pedestal, how could I mention to her the unmentionable?

My appearance among these young savages was greeted with shouts of derision. I was like a lamb at the mercy of a pack of wolves. My ignorance, my physical weakness, made me the butt of most of the older boys. The record of the humiliation and physical bullying I endured during my two first years at school is still branded on my memory. I had no one to turn to. My mother had obtained from me a promise that I should make good, and I was determined to hide from her the persecutions I had to suffer. The masters seemed unapproachable; besides, any complaint to that quarter would have made matters infinitely worse. I soon realized that I had to rely on my wits, and that my only means of escape was to howl with the pack, to gain the "friendship" of one or two strong boys by bribing them with small presents, and to pretend to be worse than the worst.

This first contact with reality showed me that I had hitherto lived in a dream and, although I refused to admit it to myself for a long time, I nursed a grievance against those who had foisted that dream upon me. When could I find truth, beauty and goodness in this merciless cynical world upon which I had been thrown, unarmed and un-prepared? What remained of my conscience but a tangle of vain self-reproach? All I wished to do was to save my pride by keeping my secret from my friends at home, and to play my game at school so skilfully that my school-fellows would be taken in. I played it so well that in the upper form I was recognized as a ringleader, a cynic of the first water. My imagination served me well in this sinister comedy, but the actor absorbed some of the vices of the character he impersonated. It was the price I had to pay.

.   .   .   .   .

It would be ungrateful of me to say that none of my masters exerted any good influence on my moral develop-ment. One or two realized their responsibility, but they were paralysed by the fear of provoking criticism. As servants of the State, they were supposed to observe a purely neutral attitude in religious and moral questions. Had they overstepped the limits placed on their activity, they might have been taxed with using their prestige with the boys to political or religious ends. Most of them played for safety and avoided all digression which might have led to controversy. Only one, a sixth-form master, dared to break the rule. He did it openly in a remarkable speech delivered at the beginning of the first term:

"I am an old man," he told us, "and have no ambition. I am too independent to rise to a headmastership. I shall, therefore, discharge my duties without regard for the consequences. Most of you are unbelievers, while I am a strong believer and feel compelled to obey orders given to me by someone who stands far above the Minister of Education. Whenever I shall feel prompted in explaining a Greek or Latin text or in discussing an essay with you, to give you what I consider a sound piece of advice about your future conduct in life, I shall not fail to do so. I am not paid to teach you either politics or religion, but I am paid to *educate* you, that is to guide you, and I warn you beforehand that I shall prove a fearless shepherd. If anybody here objects to my remarks, he is at liberty to report me and I dare say I shall suffer the consequences . . . Now, pick up your Illiad and let's begin."

From that moment a tacit pact was concluded between us. He soon gained our complete confidence, and we did not hesitate to discuss with him some of our difficulties. I remember an occasion when, in answer to a question on one of the Horace Odes, he was engaged in explaining to us the physical and moral advantages we should reap if we preserved our chastity until marriage. In the midst of the digression, the State Inspector entered our form room, followed by the Headmaster. With the utmost calm and to the complete satisfaction of the visitors, our master proceeded to question us on the poem we were translating. As soon as they retired, he picked up the thread of his talk as if nothing had happened to interrupt it.

He did not live long enough to see the results of his efforts, but some of the seeds he sowed fell on good ground. He succeeded at least in showing me that my mother's moral attitude was not so remote from reality as I had first imagined, and in giving me my first feeling of admiration for a faith which I had hitherto despised.

II

To-day, the only positive conception of life which can be opposed to Christianity is atheistic materialism, either in its capitalistic or communistic form, but in the nineteenth century the division was not so clear-cut. In non-Catholic countries, Christianity degenerated into a liberal Christianity which preserved the form of religion while neglecting most of its substance. In formerly Catholic countries, the opponents of the Church, while rejecting all its external forms of worship, endeavoured to preserve some of its moral principles.

Plato and Aristotle had already left to Christianity the four cardinal virtues of Wisdom, Justice, Temperance and Fortitude, to which St. Augustine, quoting St. Paul, had added the three theological virtues of Faith, Hope and Charity. Modern philosophy, however, discarded this inheritance, not so much because it was too closely related to Christianity, but because it could not easily be adapted to the spirit of the time.

Borrowing from the same fruitful source of Greek Philosophy, they emphasized the connection which could be established between Beauty and Goodness and completed the trinity by introducing Truth, to which they gave a very different meaning from the one given by Socrates (knowledge) and by St. Paul (divine wisdom). It would take too long to explain how these modern *values* gradually replaced the classical and mediaeval *virtues*, but this substitution should nevertheless be mentioned because it has had far more important results on the development of modern thought than is generally believed.

One of the philosophers who rendered the "values" popular on the continent in the last century was Victor Cousin. He was a *"spiritualiste,"* which does not mean that he believed in the materialisation of the spirit after death, but that he upheld the idea of duality of soul and body, spirit and matter. According to him, the spirit of man was ruled, or should be ruled, by three principles, the three eternal values of Truth, Beauty and Goodness. He defended this theory on rational grounds with many arguments which had some success among free-thinkers.

Truth, Beauty and Goodness became for them and for most liberal writers a useful screen behind which they could hide their attachment to moral principles, without incurring the suspicion of being religiously inclined. They disclaimed all belief in Jesus, at least as Christ, but claimed that the three values contained the essence of His teaching. No one could sneer at them for saying that it was right to be truthful and good and that it was wrong to be deceitful and bad. Some of the followers of this school were idealists who realized that there was something noble and disinterested in human nature which it was their task to protect against utilitarian philosophy. Others, no doubt, felt that, unless some ideals were preserved, law would lose its prestige, and that the privileged position they occupied in the State would be threatened. This explains the fact that, when Marxism entered the political arena on the continent, at the end of the century, it was attacked not only by Catholics of all classes, on religious and traditional gorunds, but also by Liberals, on philosophical grounds. Free-thinkers had been ready to destroy the Church, because it represented for them either the abuses of the Old Regime or the shackling of free criticism, but they refused to take part in the destruction of the Christian tradition, in the form of philosophical morality, as long as the preservation of this morality appeared necessary to the maintenance of a social order over which they held sway.

. . . . .

The philosophy of values failed to rally the people in the countries where it was not supported by Christian faith, because it could not be defended without it.[1]

There is no particular reason why men should sacrifice their material interests or their lust for power for the sake of abstractions. It is not surprising that a love for truth, and for beautiful and good things, and a corresponding distaste for untruth, ugly and bad things, should come naturally to people whose family tradition is deeply rooted in Christianity, even after they had lost their faith. But family tradition soon loses its hold. The son of a devout mother may allow his wife to bring up her children in the Christian faith on the ground that "women need religion." Her grandson may confine himself to bringing up his family in the observance of certain moral rules. In the third generation these rules will become mere conventions and fear of scandal. In the fourth, they will disappear altogether or be replaced by loyalties to some political party or secular creed.

In so far as the three values had a moral meaning and influenced human conduct, they could not be defended by

[1] Modern theologians have partly succeeded in defending the values on that ground, while recognising that the interpretation of Truth and Beauty leads to some confusion.

rational arguments alone. Reason which was first used in order to establish them was, at a later date, used to attack the frail metaphysical structure on which they rested. Belief in the existence of the human soul can only be explained by belief in the existence of God; it cannot be based on rational or on scientific grounds. The idea that man should be truthful, care for beautiful things and lead a good life rests on the conviction that these precepts depend on some supernatural authority. It must lose its meaning unless this authority is constantly reasserted.

The values were probably chosen because they could be connected with Christian teaching and because it was hoped that they would benefit from the connection. But this new trinity was only a sickly reflection of the uncompromising trinity of Faith, Hope and Charity, and could not be founded on early Christian tradition.[2]

If there is no divine authority, man can only rely on himself to discover the principles which must rule his conduct and, left to himself, he will ultimately follow his own interests. Truth, Beauty and Goodness will in time lose the absolute value or meaning given them; they will acquire a purely relative value and their meaning will vary according to circumstances. They will become the truth, the beauty and the goodness of the individual or the group concerned, and will not necessarily correspond to the same abstract qualities according to another individual or group. They will become attractive names given to entirely different things, like labels stuck on bottles, artificial virtues covering a multitude of sins.

This diluted morality must necessarily lead to conflict. People often quarrel when they oppose one idea to another. Their differences cannot be resolved when both sides give the same name to two totally different things.

[2] Neither Truth, nor Life, have any meaning in the Gospel apart from Christ. He is the Way, the Truth and the Life.

Diversity of opinion may be tolerated; the reproach of hypocrisy is intolerable.

An ideal society should be based on a perfect balance between individual freedom and social discipline. Men generally rely on moral principles to restore the balance, if the tendency towards individual liberty or social restriction threatens it. The three mediaeval virtues of Faith, Hope and Charity translated these two tendencies in moral terms. Men shared the same faith, that is to say were bound to obey the same commandments, and the essential commandments aimed at obtaining freedom from this world through the exercise of free will, in hope, and at loving God, and their neighbour under God, in charity. The three liberal virtues did not possess this united character; they lent themselves to purely individualistic interpretations. Truth, in its moral sense, was soon restricted to individual sincerity, beauty to individual taste, and goodness to individual tolerance or generosity.

The looseness of such morality was all the more dangerous that it was supposed to control a political and economic world in which individual liberty was overemphasized and led to disastrous abuse. In order to prevent excessive competition and exploitation of the poor by the rich, the modern world needed a far sterner discipline than the Middle Ages. The rejection of divine authority and judgment and the denial of sin favoured the adoption of principles which did not enforce this discipline. As the meaning of these abstract principles became more and more confused, their influence decreased, and the Christian inheritance was wasted in vapid oratory. Agnosticism brought about, in certain countries, complete scepticism leading to a corrupt democracy, and, in others, a materialistic reaction leading to a totalitarian regime. Morality, even in those countries which retained their constitutional traditions, became purely negative, being restricted to a healthy respect for the civil and criminal law. In totalitarian States its positive character degenerated into servile obedience to the decrees imposed by the majority or by those who had seized the reins of power. Nothing could be true, beautiful and good but what the dictator proclaimed true, beautiful and good.

The ambition of turning Man into God which haunted the minds of the Jacobins of the French Revolution had at last been realized, but the result came as a shock and a surprise to the most liberal humanists. For the vision which confronted them was not the glorification of liberty, but the glorification of slavery. It was not individual man, freed from superstitions, mastering the bland forces of nature; it was whole nations enslaved to the power of men worshipped and obeyed as God has never been obeyed since the early days of Christendom.

. . . . . .

The choice of Truth, Beauty and Goodness as the ruling values was significant, not only because it lent itself to an individualistic interpretation and favoured the exclusion of supernatural authority, but also because it reflected the blind confidence which Liberalism placed in secular education.

On the continent, and particularly in Catholic countries, education had been the monopoly of the religious orders since the Middle Ages. By influencing the youth, the Church of Rome had regained, in the seventeenth and eighteenth centuries, a good deal of the ground it had lost at the time of the Reformation. Liberal governments, after freeing trade from state control, applied themselves to the "emancipation" of education from religious control. They were, however, hampered in their efforts by the very doctrine they upheld. Practically every liberal constitution framed after 1830 guaranteed freedom of worship as well as freedom of teaching, and it proved difficult to remove the schools from clerical influence without violating these fundamental principles.

Most liberal idealists considered that the school should replace the Church and that the teacher was destined to supersede the priest. This was the logical consequence of a secular outlook. It was agreed that man was essentially good, but it could not be denied that he did not always behave as he should. These errors were attributed to the reactionary influences, symbolised in the countryside by "the castle and the church." They could only be corrected by an education which would develop the child's "innate goodness."

Laissez faire, laissez passer, in economics and politics, corresponded to *laissez penser* in education. It was believed that the nature of man must necessarily progress under the influence of free speech and a free press, among the adults, and a secular education among the young. Free thinkers realized with more sense than many Christians that religion, being based on revelation, must necessarily be dogmatic and that the acceptance of dogma and divine authority must escape scientific analysis. In England, the conflict in education was, as usual, resolved in compromise, but in most continental countries it led to a bitter struggle and, in Germany and France, to open persecution.

The prevalent opinion was that only an education freed from dogmatic restrictions could develop the spirit of Truth and Beauty in the child and release his natural Goodness. Liberal governments provided funds for the foundation of a number of schools and universities. These subsidies placed religious and private schools at a disadvantage and, apart from a few countries where Catholicism was deeply rooted among an agricultural population, the scope of religious teaching was pitifully reduced. The advent of liberal education led, paradoxically enough, to the adoption of the principle of compulsion and, in some countries, state interference was strengthened to such an extent as to encroach upon the freedom of the teacher, and turn the school into a powerful instrument of political propaganda. In escaping from the domination of the Church, education became more and more dominated by the State.

.   .   .   .

To-day we should be in a position to appreciate how far the expectations based on secular education have been fulfilled.

The ideal was to correct man's errors and improve his nature through the teaching of Truth and Beauty, of science and arts. After every disappointment in internal or external affairs, we were told that it was due to the ignorance of a rapidly growing electorate. Education had not kept pace with the extension of the suffrage. When it did, Progress and Enlightenment would walk hand in hand.

Concerning Truth, a curious confusion arose between moral and scientific truth, knowledge and sincerity. It was assumed that a learned man must necessarily be sincere and therefore virtuous. This confusion was no doubt due to the fact that a historian or a scientist must entertain a healthy respect for the accurate record of facts and experiments, if he is to win any reputation. Charlatans are not generally popular in university circles. But the fact that you are not a charlatan does not necessarily make you a good or sincere man.

What applies to teachers applies with greater force to the students and with still greater force to the general public. The opinion according to which the moral quality of men and women depends on the advancement of their studies or on their academic qualifications has lost a great deal of its former prestige to-day. No serious moral discrimination can be made between men and women on the grounds of learning, not even on the grounds of intelligence, which is by no means the same thing. What is true is that education, when it succeeds in developing intelligence, may increase the power for good or evil which every one possesses, while ignorance restricts this power. Knowledge is an instrument which may be beneficent or harmful. It all depends on the quality of the person who wields it.

In the last century no country in Europe was more admired for its learning than Germany. German popular schools and methods of teaching were upheld as examples. German universities acquired such a reputation that no university training appeared complete unless the promising student finished his studies in one of them. Now that the tree can be judged by its fruit, it has become the fashion to criticize the German system of education and to proclaim that the systems adopted elsewhere could not lead to the same disasters. But it was not so much the tree which was wrong as the soil on which the tree grew. It was not the German system of education which was the main cause of Germany's moral decadence, it was the fact that the German people were not politically minded, and that no amount of scientific and artistic education can replace a strong political tradition. France possessed a very fine educational system, but that system did not save her from the disastrous consequences of political corruption. England, on the other hand, had preserved her public spirit based on religious tradition, and the fact that the State exerted only a minimum of control on the strange and confused medley of schools and universities where her young people pursued their studies did not prevent her from weathering the storm.

Secular education cannot transform the soul of a people.

At its highest level, it develops both intelligence and sensitiveness. If the moral foundation is sound, it may therefore succeed in making it sounder, but if it is unsound or if it rests on the shifting sand of doubt, it will only accelerate the process of disintegration by encouraging destructive thought or by creating mass hysteria. It is significant that German education was inclined, on the one hand, to emphasize criticism and, on the other, to stimulate sentiment.

Truly Christian education develops both reason and faith, the mind and the heart. It brings together and harmonizes human faculties. But secular education is apt to separate these faculties and to foster, at the same time, a harsh intellectual attitude and an over-excitable enthusiasm. It is dangerous to pass abruptly from the strain of Hegel's metaphysics to the strain of Wagnerian or post-Wagnerian music.

.   .   .   .

It might be objected that the liberal experiment was not conclusive because it never was given sufficient scope to fulfil its purpose.

Even if a part of the teaching given in modern secular schools develops the mind its influence is restricted by the necessity of equipping the scholars for adult life, that is to say, of providing them with the qualifications which will allow them to practise a certain trade or profession. This involves a fixed curriculum in all schools, and "cramming" for examinations. The main conditions of success are a good memory, speed, and neatness of expression. None of these conditions demands a particularly intelligent mind, still less a particularly truthful or sensitive character.

The materialistic character of modern society is also responsible for the neglect of Beauty. The teaching of art in secondary schools is practically negligible, and is no preparation for the appreciation of the masterpieces of painting, sculpture or architecture. The result of the teaching of literature is generally to inspire the young with a distaste for poetry and for the few "set books" they are compelled to study. This failure is due partly to bad teaching and partly to the present system of examinations. But it is mainly due to the utilitarian trend of modern education which it would be far more difficult to alter.

It is this drive towards efficiency which the advocates of secular education forgot to take into account when they made their grandiose plans for the conversion of the world through Truth, Beauty and Goodness. A secular education must sooner or later be dominated by secular interests, the conquest of certificates and degrees, the equipment of the young for the "battle of life." An utilitarian outlook leads to the neglect of everything which does not achieve "concrete results." That is why so much attention is paid to-day to technology, medicine and economics, and so little to art, literature and philosophy. That is also why the study of modern languages is being gradually substituted for that of the so-called "dead languages." Even in university circles, we meet again and again the familiar argument: "Why should the student spend so much time on subjects which will be of no use to him in later years?" The gospel of "eternal values" is rapidly making way for the gospel of efficiency. The educationalist is no longer preoccupied with those things which are "good for the soul" or even for the mind, but with those things which are likely to provide a substantial return in the form of salary.

Recent developments seem to show that an important change is taking place in several countries where the idea of "social service" is substituted for the idea of "private income," and the welfare of the community for the comfort of the individual. In socialistic States, new subjects are being introduced in the upper forms, such as elementary notions of law, politics and economics, for the purpose of giving the scholar a "social sense" and of preparing him to exercise his rights and fulfil his duties as a citizen. But the philosophy which inspires this new form of education is as materialistic and utilitarian as that which ruined the idealistic schemes of Liberalism. The only difference is that the interest of the community or of the party which rules it, takes the place of the interest of the individual. What is meant by a "good citizen" is not necessarily a good man, but only a man useful to the State. Both capitalists and socialists are opposed to "useless" studies, such as that of the classics, and are determined to eliminate them from the curriculum.

The last defenders of liberal values and of a "disinterested education" are no longer able to resist the increasing pressure brought upon them. We are gradually driven to a situation when a choice will have to be made between the reality of atheistic materialism and the reality of Christianity.

. . . . . .

One of the best guides towards the understanding of possible reforms is perhaps the Norwood report on secondary education, published in England, in July 1943.

The authors reject the suggestion that "the aim of education can be dictated by the provisional findings of special sciences, whether biological, psychological, or sociological," and that its function is "to fit pupils to determine their outlook and conduct according to the changing needs and changing standards of the day." They are neither narrowly individualistic nor narrowly socialistic, and attempt to strike an even balance between the "intellectual, aesthetic, spiritual and physical wants of the pupils," and their future needs "as citizens in a society of fellow citizens and fellow workers." In order to achieve this result, they suggest a number of reforms which might to a certain extent relieve the mind of teacher and scholar of the obsession of examinations.

The report reacts at one and the same time against materialistic education, and the sentimental idea that the one task of all teachers is to give scope to the free development of the personality of his pupil. For "human personality contains many possibilities; some are worthy to be developed, some are not; the task of education is to develop those which are worthy and good and to control those which are unworthy and base." This is in complete contradition to a number of theories favoured during the last hundred years. A moral choice has to be made and this choice must derive from some unchallengeable authority. The reader expects to find in this part of the report a plain statement that God Himself is the judge of human destiny and that any guidance the teacher may give must be based on divine authority. It is therefore disappointing to discover that the authors fall back on the nineteenth century values. "We believe," they write, "that education cannot stop short of recognising the ideal of truth, beauty and goodness as final and binding for all times and in all places, as ultimate values . . ." But they add: "Further, we hold that the recognition of such values implies, for most people at least, a religious interpretation of life which for us means the Christian interpretation of life."

The Norwood report, while revealing the fact that religious education is at present "confined to one period a week" and that only a minority of those who teach "religious knowledge" in secondary schools are even fairly well qualified for their work, suggests devoting twice this amount of time to Scripture and placing religious education, as distinct from Scripture, "outside and above the curriculum, being the concern of all teachers at all stages," on the ground that "religious consciousness grows from the environment, *favourably and naturally if the environment is favourable and natural, atrophied and distorted if the environment is materialistic in its values, and purely competitive in spirit.* It is a growth from a life that is lived.

A long time passes between the publication of a report and the application of its conclusions to social life.[3] Much remains to be done in connecting once more eternal values and principles with the spirit of the Gospel on which they are supposed to be based. If the present progress continues, it may one day become possible to state boldly, even in official reports, that the most important task of education, in all its stages and in all its aspects, is the development of knowledge and character in the service and worship of God.

. . . . .

Even if Liberal educationalist had been able to train competent teachers, free to deal with their subject without being hampered at every step by the curriculum, and to outline a plan of studies aiming only at developing the pupil's intelligence and sense of appreciation, their success would have been more than doubtful. For it depended on the idea that intellectual or artistic progress necessarily implies a higher standard of morality. In fact, Truth and Beauty bring with them a richer life, perhaps a fuller life, more intelligence and sensitivity, but not a better life.

[3] A comparison between the Norwood report and the new Educational Bill shows the obstacles which must still be overcome, particularly when the different denominations are taken into account. The undertaking of excluding "any catechism or formularly distinctive of any particular denomination" is significant (*White Paper*, 24).

The nineteenth century idealists missed the connecting link between the three values, and they were bound to miss it, because the connecting link is the love of God expressed in Faith, Hope and Charity.

There is a fourteenth century fresco, in the Spanish Chapel of Santa Maria Novella, in Florence, in which the seven temporal and sacred arts and sciences are represented, sitting on carved thrones, while the three theological Virtues hover above them in heaven. If a similar fresco were painted to-day, the artist would no doubt depart from the *trivium* and *quadrivium* which Thomas Aquinas expounded in his *Summa*, but unless he showed by some plain symbol that the human search for knowledge depends for its fruitfulness on the love of God, his work would remain both incomplete and misleading.

Given the love of God, there is no limit to man's fruitful activity in his search for Truth and Beauty. Goodness should not have come last in the trinity, it should have come first, like Faith. For it is not the consequence of man's spiritual development; it is its essential condition.

A writer or an artist is not only the servant of Literature or Art, or even of Beauty, he is also the servant of Good or Evil, even when he writes a novel or paints a landscape. It is not only what he does that matters, but also the spirit in which he does it, and the influence which this spirit exercises upon others.

.   .   .   .   .

In education or in politics and economics, there is no way back. For better or for worse, liberal humanism has drawn every body into political life, enforced compulsory education, and covered the land with workshops and factories. The shape of civilisation has been altered and the old order of things cannot be restored, not only because its restoration would mean famine and revolution, but also because its defects have been made so apparent as to obscure its qualities. There is no way back, as far as external forms are concerned, but there are stepping stones leading across the flood to a less wasteful industrialism and a more educated democracy. Popular education is a necessary adjunct to popular politics, but this education, in order to be effective, must be pre-eminently moral and therefore religious. To neglect the moral training of the young is to neglect to clean a glass before filling it with wine. The best wine will lose its flavour if the glass has been left dirty.

Goodness should come first, like Faith, not merely a sentimental goodness fostering humane ideals, but a righteous Goodness inspired by the love of God, like ancient Charity, who consumes in her fire both evil and injustice. It is only when man's soul has been purged of sin, when in every school, lay or religious teachers become, not merely useful "crammers," but good men whose example inspires affection and respect, that scientific or artistic knowledge may achieve its end. Science and art may then open the scholar's mind, increase his strength and sensitivity, and his power to do good.

There is no way back, but there is a way across, not through less education of the wrong kind, but through more education of the right kind. The knowledge of God is the only sure foundation on which the knowledge of nature and man can be built. The fragile edifice erected by the nineteenth century idealists and destroyed by the twentieth century realists, may be built once more. But this time the corner stone must not be forgotten.

III.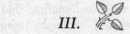

THE LIMITS OF FREEDOM

I

WHEN I WAS A YOUNG STUDENT IN BRUSSELS, I KNEW A GREAT worshipper of mankind. He was a French writer well-known in the nineties as the author of a large geographical encyclopaedia written in excellent prose. Those who liked Elysée Reclus called him the Michelet of geography, those who disliked him denounced him as an anarchist leader. Being a passionate individualist, he would have refused to be called a leader, for he believed that every man should lead himself. Neither would he have admitted that he belonged to a party, for anything which savoured of organisation, especially political organisation, was repulsive to him. To express myself accurately, I should say that he was one of the revolutionists who, with Prince Kropotkin, then exiled in London, had seceded from the First International at the time of the quarrel between Marx and Bakunin, and who preached the gospel of social revolution in their lectures and articles, without adopting the more violent methods of Russian terrorism.

Reclus had the personality of a Victorian prophet, but his ideas would have shocked the boldest Victorian. Short of stature, he bore on his square shoulders a leonine head surrounded by a halo of white hair. He had the proud assurance of an experienced traveller who had wandered through the world and overcome many obstacles. He scorned fear like a Spanish grandee, and combined a well-informed love of nature with a fierce passion for the

47

Social Revolution. When he spoke of the oppressors of the people, his grey eyes shone with indignation, but when he mentioned "*les temps nouveaux*," his husky voice broke under the strain of emotion. He was deeply sincere and his enthusiasm was contagious. I caught the contagion myself and embraced the new uncompromising doctrine which denounced God, the State, marriage and property.

Even in those days, I wondered how a man who had reached the age of seventy, after acquiring a personal knowledge of so many lands and fighting the "good fight" since the days of the French Commune, could preserve so many illusions. But I admired him for it. He was right in being wrong, because his errors sprang from a blind faith not only in mankind, but in every man he met—as long as he was not a "bourgeois" or a politician. I had always been troubled by the contradictory declarations of socialist leaders. They paid lip service to the Revolution, but accepted the parliamentary system and urged certain reforms which, by appeasing the people's grievances, could only postpone the final outbreak. They denied evil, at least among the working classes, but maintained and even reinforced the machinery of the State which would become useless as soon as men were "free to be good." In short, they were opportunists and I hated opportunism.

I had been brought up on Rousseau's doctrines and I found in Reclus a true Rousseauist, truer than Rousseau himself. His logic was devastating. If we deny God and original sin, and lay all crimes at the door of "oppression," priests, judges and policemen become more than useless. The removal of all forms of control is bound to liberate those beneficent forces which must bring about universal peace and content. The existence of the State itself will be superfluous, for if all individuals wish to do the right thing towards the community, a spontaneous organisation will gradually emerge from the apparent disorder, and no sanctions will be required to maintain it. There were some discussions about salaries, and who would pay them, and whether they would be paid in money or in kind. Salaries of course there must be, even if the work was not adequate. To the Socialist formula: "To everybody according to his work," we opposed the more radical formula: "To everybody according to his wants."

All this may seem very strange to-day, but it did not sound so strange forty or fifty years ago. Such ideas were ridiculed by the Conservatives, but so were many social reforms which were adopted under pressure, a few years later, by the same Conservatives. Society was sharply divided and the advanced parties, intoxicated by recent scientific discoveries, considered progress as inevitable. This belief tallied with many vague notions applying to human history the theory of natural evolution and adaptation to surroundings. The "social organism" would grow from strength to strength, like the human organism, from the embryo to the adult stage. Its beginning was in the family, "the original cell," its full development in a society embracing the whole world, without distinction of class, race, or nations. Cities, kingdoms, continental federations were only stages on the road. Human knowledge increased with the size of the social unit. Some "sociologists" were already seeking the mathematical formula of human development and hoped to solve the "equation of human happiness."

These theories were only mentioned with some reluctance by Reclus and his disciples, because strict determinism was in contradiction with their belief in the virtue of individual freedom, but this minor difficulty did not diminish their faith in scientific achievements. We felt with some reason that we were living on the brink of catastrophic events. We had doubts about the precise nature of the catastrophe and about the steps to be taken after it had occurred, but since the future was bound to be better than the past, we set our shoulders to the wheel with all our might in order to hasten the pace of time. We all hoped to live long enough to see the Revolution. Some of us lived long enough to see the Great War.

. . . . . .

The fact is that the Revolution was in those days the religion of a large number of people, not only among the industrial classes, but also among the young bourgeois. They believed in it as the early Christians believed in the Second Advent. They discussed it and quarrelled about it, quoting freely from Marx, Engels, Bakunin, and Proudhon. This religion had its prophets, its apostles, its martyrs and its heretics. Enthusiasm ran so high that the members of one sect professed a far deeper antagonism towards the members of a rival sect than towards the "powers of reaction." The latter were merely the enemies of to-day, the former the enemies of to-morrow. Having renounced for good every belief in the supernatural, the revolutionists projected all their longing for certainty, their yearning for perfection, into Nature and Man. There was nothing wrong in the impulse, but there was something radically wrong in its direction. The engine had run off the rails and the train was bound to follow. The religious instinct is so deeply ingrained in the nature of man that, if it is suppressed in one sphere of activity, where it can be fruitful, it is bound to manifest itself in another, where it will bring about disaster. Voltaire remarked with some cynicism that "if God did not exist, we should have to invent him." A century later, revolutionists declared that since Paradise did not exist in heaven, it should be realized on earth. The conquests of Science, the exploration of the remotest regions of the world, the triumphs of democracy were sure omens of its coming.

Reclus' faith was a perfect example of this kind of social mysticism which has flourished since all over Europe in strange and unexpected forms. He was the son of a stern Calvinist minister who had inherited a good deal of the puritan fanaticism of the old huguenot of Southern France. This worthy man had ruled his large family with a rod of iron and most of his children had waited impatiently for the day when they could shake off the yoke which weighed so heavily on their shoulders. They had renounced God and every kind of authority, but had preserved nevertheless a good deal of the puritanism which had darkened their youth.

Reclus used to declare that it was a dangerous delusion for an anarchist to wait for the revolution before conforming his life to his principles, and he was as good as his word. Fortunately, since his wife did not share his views, he was not deprived of the necessaries of life, but these were reduced to an uncomfortable minimum. He combined his worship of man with a worship of life, and followed a strict vegetarian diet—so strict, that eggs had to be tested before they appeared on the table. He wore felt boots instead of leather ones, shunned tobacco, and never touched wine or beer. Although his means were very restricted, his generosity was so well known that no revolutionist, genuine or not, passed through Brussels without calling on him for help.

I often wondered how he was able to work, considering that his door remained open to all visitors day and night. I never came to see him without meeting some "comrade" in his room, or at the door. No particulars were asked by the members of the family who answered the bell. You were shown in, and walked up two flights of stairs until you reached the small room where the geographer sat at a deal table, surrounded by a large number of cardboard boxes in which he filed his documents with meticulous care. He stopped writing the moment you entered, and finished the sentence after saying good-bye. On certain occasions, the practice of communism caused some inconvenience to the household. Umbrellas, coats and hats disappeared from the hall or were replaced by some shabby garment worn by the visitor, so great was the latter's faith that the "master," as he was sometimes called to his great disgust, would not resent the exchange. Within one week, I saw him wearing two different hats which did not suit him at all. Upon enquiry, he explained that some of his friends must have been in great need of headgear lately, and that he had not been able to procure a suitable one in time.

I helped him in the distribution of a series of pamphlets which he had printed at his own expense, and we were frequently short of money. I volunteered to make a collection among our friends and apologized for not being able to add my own contribution being at the time particularly hard up. He pointed to the pipe I was smoking:

"How much do you spend on tobacco?" he asked.

"Between two and three francs each month."

"How much did you spend on tram fares to-day?"

"Twenty centimes."

"Don't smoke, and walk. It will do you good and we shall get a regular contribution of over a hundred francs per year."

Such was his magnetism that I followed his suggestion, if not for years, at least for months.

If the man had been born in the Middle Ages, he might have been called a saint. Being born in the nineteenth century, he was an outcast who had only escaped deportation in 1871 owing to the intervention of his scientific colleagues, and who was obliged to spend the last years of his life in exile. This was not entirely the fault of the society in which he lived, it was also the fault of the theories which he professed. His creed, as far as he was concerned, left him free to do what he thought to be good; but that same creed justified the worst abuses in others, the quality of freedom in this world varying according to the character of the man who exerts it.

Had I been as disinterested as he was, our friendship might have lasted to the end of his life. It was not the disparity of age which caused the breach, for he was almost as young at seventy as I was at twenty, and he possessed a strong sense of humour in spite of his austerity. He never caused me any disillusion, being the most consistent and righteous being I ever met. But I made the cardinal mistake of taking him at his word. When he called me his friend, sometimes his "dear friend," I imagined that he gave to this expression, which he used lavishly—since, in fact, all men were his friends—the same meaning which I gave to it. I did not regret the sacrifices which I made to "the cause," but I expected to get something in return. I had severed myself from many family friends who took strong exception to my views and to the kind of life I was leading, and I felt somewhat lonely. In the circumstances, I thought I might claim the affection of the man whose influence had caused these difficulties. When I sought his advice and help, he listened patiently, as he listened to all who appealed to him, even to those whom I thought did not deserve his attention. But I wished for something more, something which it was neither in his nature nor in his power to give me. I also noticed that his interest in me depended too much on our common belief in the same political ideal. As soon as I became critical and questioned some of his dogmas, which as a "free individual" I was entitled to do, I felt that he made no effort to understand my attitude. He first tried to persuade me that I was wrong, but when he failed the bond was loosened. I began to wonder if he liked me for myself or for the ideas I shared with him.

"Reclus," I had been warned by a mutual friend, "is incapable of affection. It is the last thing you should ask from him. Like Pygmalion, he has carved a fine marble statue which he calls mankind, and while he is worshipping it he allows real men and women to pass by unnoticed."

Several years after our last meeting during which I had vainly tried to explain myself to him, I learnt that he was gravely ill. I felt a pang of remorse and brought him, as a token of reconciliation, a valuable book which I knew he had long wished to acquire. He was sitting in an armchair from which he was no longer able to raise himself. He received me as if nothing had happened between us. "You know," he remarked before I left him, "I still do not understand why we have not seen each other for so long."

It was our last meeting. A few days later, in July, 1905, the papers published the news that an insurrection had broken out in St. Petersburg. This was his death-blow. Overjoyed, he stood up and shouted in a last outburst of energy: "Long live the Russian Revolution!" then fell back never to rise again.

II

Both Christianity and Humanism declare that the exercise of freedom is the condition of moral responsibility. But while the Christian maintains that freedom should be restricted to the liberty of choosing between right and wrong, between obedience or disobedience to God, the humanist has always insisted on the fact that freedom was good in itself and that its exercise was only limited by the necessity of respecting the freedom of others. This difference is the logical consequence of the first principle of humanistic philosophy which is based on the essential goodness of Man. If man is good, any restriction placed on the expression of his personality or activity must be detrimental to progress. If he is at the same time good and bad, his good faculties should be developed and his bad faculties restrained by some authority.

The Christian agrees with the humanist that, if this authority is purely temporal, it must necessarily become arbitrary and lead to abuse. But while the humanist, in order to safeguard freedom, is obliged to declare that discipline is only temporary, and to look forward to a utopian future when it can be totally removed, the Christian believes that discipline is indispensable to individual and social existence and can only be removed when it is absorbed into the love of God and the perfect obedience to His Commandments. The love of mankind can never prevent a rivalry of interests and aspirations between individuals, classes and nations, and the only means of checking constant conflicts is to subordinate these interests and aspirations to a national or international authority which, being human, must always be defective and appear arbitrary. The love of God implies the duty of sacrificing all competition to a supernatural authority which, being perfect, cannot infringe upon freedom, that is to say upon the free choice between good and evil. While therefore freedom and love can never be reconciled in the natural world, they can be and are reconciled in this supernatural world, in the kingdom of God. The humanist will always seek in a remote future the realisation of his ideal, the Christian can find it here and now, in his relationship with Christ.

Once we accept this transcendent love and authority, the Christian attitude is strictly consistent. If we reject them, the only logical attitude is that professed, a century ago, by Bakunin and his intellectual disciples, such as Reclus and Kropotkin. The anarchist is the only consistent humanist. For him, Man is indeed God and any limitation placed on the exercise of freedom is a blasphemous desecration. Every action is justified if it aims at breaking the moral and physical obstacles which prevent the individual from saying and doing what he likes. Patriotism, property, marriage, must be sacrificed on the altar of this ruthless secular religion. The right to happiness through freedom can only be conquered by removing the priest, the soldier and the policeman. Order can only be restored through the elimination of all constituted authority, spiritual or temporal, national or international, and must find its foundation in the pressure of public opinion which should persuade any recalcitrant individual not to harm the interests of the community.

This movement which was very active in Czarist Russia and manifested itself as late as the Spanish civil war, has often been underestimated. Its doctrine, compared with Christianity, is at the opposite pole of human philosophy, but its position, compared with that of Liberalism, Socialism and Communism, remains a very strong one. The anarchist will always be able to point out that he is at least faithful to the fundamental principles of Humanism, as proclaimed by the American and French Revolutions, and to argue that if these principles had not been betrayed, they might have borne fruit. He declares that Liberalism failed because it protected the abuses of Capitalism instead of denouncing them, that Socialism failed because it compromised with a corrupt parliamentary system, and that even the Russian revolution failed because the dictatorship of the proletariat is incompatible with human liberty. He has no difficulty in showing that in postponing the date at which the aims of the Revolution could be realized and enforcing meanwhile a transitory regime inconsistent with these aims, those revolutionary movements rendered the advent of Utopia impossible.

What the anarchist will not recognize is that Liberalism, Socialism and Communism found themselves compelled to enforce order in this way because, men being what they are, no order is possible without authority, and that the most imperfect regime is better than disorder, i.e. anarchy. The worshipper of man and nature cannot be expected to admit that unrestrained freedom must lead to lawlessness and lawlessness to the struggle for existence and the survival of the fittest, to the lowering of social life from the human to the natural standard.

It is significant that the ideal of total freedom should have been formulated when Humanism began to assert itself, at the time of the Renaissance. It appears, for the first time, in the writings of Moore, Erasmus and Rabelais. This modern freedom should not be confused with the individual freedom of the pagan philosophers, especially of the stoics, which, instead of leading man back to nature, endeavoured to raise him above the natural world of caprice and passions. There is a world of difference between the strict control exercised by Socrates upon himself, and the golden rule of the Thelemites, as propounded by Rabelais in his Gargantua: *Fay ce que voudras.* It is true that the sixteenth century humanists only apply their principles to an aristocracy which, through a careful education, had already been trained not to abuse the liberty granted them, but they insist nevertheless on the fact that restrictions "thwart the noble affections and virtues" which are natural to man and prompt him to rebel and act unsocially. "We always wish to do what is forbidden and we long to obtain what is denied to us."[1]

This is the central idea of the doctrine of modern freedom, as it is still defended to-day by some psychologists, followers of Freud. Every morbid or anti-social tendency is explained through oppression or frustration. The evil

[1] *Gargantua,* Chapter LVII.

complex can only be cured by removing its essential cause: every form of punishment. Temptation and sin are the result of restraint. Eve would never have thought of eating the apple had she not been forbidden to do so. It was therefore God, and not Satan, who tempted her. Evil as such does not exist, but frustrated goodness may produce evil results. The fact that misdirected energy is both wasteful and dangerous, is overlooked. Neither are we told why, if free self-expression always yields good results, the necessity would ever have occurred of restraining such freedom, unless the restrainer, that is all-knowing God, had wished to induce man to sin in order to be justified in punishing him. This thesis propounded by several romantic poets leads us nowhere, since it only removes evil from the satanic to the divine sphere.

The gulf which separates the Christian from the anarchist is insuperable. The Christian acknowledges sin and the dual nature of man as a fact of daily observation; he explains it by the existence of evil forces, opposed to divine wisdom and goodness, which tempt man to act against the will of God. Placed before this temptation man is left free to choose between right and wrong, because his obedience to God must be prompted by love, not by fear or any selfish motive. To obey God's commandments in order to reap any benefit in this world or in the other is to deprive oneself of such benefit. "Not everyone that saith unto me, 'Lord, Lord,' shall enter into the Kingdom of heaven . . ."

The anarchist, as the consistent humanist, refuses to acknowledge human sin, in spite of all evidence. He cannot however deny that some men, if left free, will abuse the freedom given to them, but he has such faith in the goodness of human nature that he attributes these defects solely to the restrictions imposed by authority, whether paternal, religious or political, in order to prevent them from destroying social relations. The suppression of all authority would instantly substitute a society in which all citizens would compete with each other to serve the community, for a society in which they compete with each other to obtain personal advantages. To quote Rabelais once more: "This freedom prompted them all to enter into a praiseworthy emulation in order to satisfy the wish of one of them. If one of them said: 'Let us drink,' they all drank. If one of them said: 'Let us play,' they all played. . . ." We are not told who provided the drinks or the food, for no Thelemite suggested that they might work.

The other modern schools of humanists whether liberal, socialistic or communistic do not go so far because they are not so consistent. While professing an unlimited confidence in the goodness of human nature and rejecting the Christian conception of evil and sin, they are not prepared to put this theory to the test. The enfranchisement of man from moral and economic shackles must be gradual. Between the reality of to-day and the utopia of to-morrow, there must be, according to them, a transitory stage during which some kind of authority must be exercised, but this authority must emanate neither from the Sovereign, nor from the State as such, but from the people themselves or from the party which has seized power.

As long as faith in the future Utopia is preserved, democracy remains in a fluid state and is susceptible of development. It possesses the qualities of a compromise, in so far as it takes into account the realities of this world and the necessity of controlling freedom. It possesses also some of its defects, because it cannot be considered as a stable regime and is constantly subjected to the criticisms of those who urge that less control should be exercised and more advantages granted in order that the promised Utopia might be sooner realized. Every government comes to power on the strength of promises which it is unable to fulfil, and falls from power because it has failed to fulfil them. When economic and political conditions are favourable these changes take place in a relatively calm atmosphere and the mirage of Utopia recedes into the background. But when conditions are unfavourable and the people are subjected to want and starvation the contrast between the mirage and hard reality becomes too blatant for faith in the future to be preserved. Despair provokes a revolution which brings about the dictatorship of any demagogue bold enough to reassert the false promise, and unscrupulous enough to put the blame for previous failures, not on its fallacy, but on the corruption and inefficiency of the government which made it.

Needless to say, the dictator will be just as incapable as the previous democratic government to give satisfaction to the people's unlimited demands; he will then attempt to cut the Gordian knot by launching his country into war. Sooner or later, this collective sin meets its retribution and the pendulum swings back in the other direction. It is difficult to imagine how these alternatives of ruthless and moderate regimes will cease to manifest themselves as long as Utopia remains the goal of human efforts.

The *Liberté, Egalité, Fraternité* of the French Revolution led to the Convention, the Napoleonic regime, Constitutional monarchy, a second spell of Imperialism, the Commune of 1871, and the Fourth Republic. Similar changes occurred recently in Italy and Germany and are likely to continue to succeed each other wherever the people are not roused from the political dreams which have engendered them.

. . . . .

No Christian, aware of the inherent imperfection of "Caesar," or any other temporal power, can identify himself with a particular political or economic system. He may, in the light of Christianity, object to one system less than to another and exercise his rights as a citizen accordingly, but his choice must always be between two evils. He recognizes at one and the same time, the existence of sin, the necessity of restraining it, and the defects of any temporal power which will restrain it. In the Middle Ages, this contradiction was so strongly felt that many Christians tried to escape from it by taking refuge in a monastery. Even there, they could not entirely evade their responsibilities, for they were dependent on the temporal power which protected them from invaders and robbers. The Christian's only means of action in this world —and he is under a moral obligation to act—is so to influence the mind of the community and of its government so that the law of the land might be improved and administered in the light of Christian principles. But he can only do so effectively if these Christian principles are recognized by the majority; which may lead him back to the slow process of evangelisation.

However unsatisfactory this method may appear to the impatient younger generation, it is infinitely preferable to the compromises of Liberal Christianity and to the confusion which prevails in certain circles between the last secular Utopia and the Kingdom of God.

You cannot prove that Christianity is right and Humanism wrong as you can prove that a mathematical proposition is right or wrong. Faith comes before reason in religion and in politics. We should however remember that the Christian faith, although supernatural, leads to a conception of the world which appears fruitful in the light of history, while every humanistic attempt at establishing human happiness on natural foundations has ended in disaster. If religious truth lies beyond the reach of reason, secular truth should be within its reach. It is therefore somewhat surprising to notice that when we apply the test of history to the first, we obtain positive results, and that when we apply the same test to the second, we obtain negative results. It is only when we assume God's existence that we are able to conduct ourselves individually and socially in a sensible manner. What has been called the mad belief in the supernatural is the only way which leads to natural sanity.

The process is not difficult to understand. The Christian is a citizen like any other citizen; he also has to earn his living, to keep his family; he also wishes to lead a peaceful life in a peaceful world. But he is less inclined to protest against the shortcomings of the society in which he lives and to seek a hasty and sometimes violent solution for his trouble in war and revolution. This patience and moderation is due to two main reasons.

The first is that the Christian conception of the world corresponds, not to a dream or Utopia, but to reality. Man being sinful, it is only normal that any government should be imperfect and that any regime should foster a certain amount of waste and corruption. The Christian's indignation will not therefore be roused whenever his personal interests are affected. He cannot claim from others a perfection which he does not possess himself. Knowing only too well his own failings and trained in the practice of private and public confession, he preserves enough humility to envisage the shortcomings of the world in which he lives without anger or impatience. That is not to say that he will not feel it his duty to protest against gross abuse which endangers Christianity or against any attack on his freedom of conscience, since the preservation of this freedom is the condition of his spiritual life. Neither can he tolerate any interference with the exercise of his worship or any restriction placed on his right to teach, write and speak in order to witness to his Lord or to spread the Gospel. He must show and he has shown with indomitable courage during the last few years, that there is no compromise possible between the Christian Church and a regime which aims at bringing back the majority of men to a state of physical and moral slavery. There are limits beyond which no concessions are possible, but within these limits the Christian cannot share the critical spirit of most of his compatriots who, convinced of their own virtue and eager to defend their "right to happiness," are always ready to attribute the worst motives to the actions of their political opponents. If he preserves a sufficient sense of his own unworthiness, he will neither be surprised or shocked at the unworthiness of others. If he realizes the part he should take in the corporate life of his Church, which includes people belonging to all races and classes, he will not be affected in his judgments by class or racial prejudices. Aware that most systems have their qualities and their defects, and that their value depends mostly on the spirit in which they are applied, he will not identify himself with any political regime. He must always be in the opposition, but his opposition must always be constructive.

Christians do not wish to remain aloof from political life, but their existence being centred on God, such life only affects them as far as it affects their relationship with Him. They are told to love their neighbour, but their sense of brotherhood depends on their filial love for God. When they see their compatriots engaged in some secular conflict, they cannot share their political fanaticism. In short, having a supernatural faith, they cannot harbour a secular one. They may strive in one direction or in another in the hope that their action may provide some improvement in social or international conditions, but they can never look upon such an improvement as upon an end in itself, because for them its value must always remain relative to moral and religious principles, and because they preserve a sense of proportion between the finite goodness of man and the infinite goodness of God.

It is sometimes contended that the patience of the Christian reveals lack of courage, and the methods pursued by liberal Christianity during the last century have done a good deal to foster this opinion. But liberal Christianity is neither sound doctrine nor sound policy. The Christianity of the Gospel exacts from us infinitely more courage than any political creed, the courage of recognizing our sins, of confessing them, of breaking, if called to do so, all human ties for the sake of God, of sacrificing possession, ambition, pride, even spiritual pride, for the drudgery of a humble life. If it is objected that this effort is made for the purpose of winning eternal life on the day of judgment, it may be answered that the greatest courage of all is perhaps to realize the necessity of that dreadful trial.

Viewed in its secular perspective, the life of the Christian in this world should appear to the unbeliever as the boldest of all gambles. For he gives up everything for the love of a God who may not exist, and for a salvation which can only be obtained if he remains conscious that he does not deserve it.

. . . . . .

There is another aspect of freedom which should be considered when we compare the secular to the Christian outlook in the modern world.

The rationalist believes that the acceptance of a dogma implies the sacrifice of intellectual freedom. On the strength that "a dogma is a truth which cannot be proved," any dogmatic philosophy of life, any rule of conduct which is not determined by scientific knowledge is, according to him, either absurd or "slavish." For a long time the name "free-thinker" was synonymous with "unbeliever." Conversely, every believer was presumed to be no longer "free" to think. In spite of the fact that some eminent scientists have joined the Church, many people are still convinced that scientific knowledge is incompatible with religious dogma.

This conviction, like most convictions dealing with the relationship between science and religion, is the result of a misunderstanding for which the attitude of the Church in the past is largely responsible. By confusing scientific and religious knowledge and persecuting the pioneers of modern science, such as Galileo, the Church committed exactly the same mistake which modern rationalists are committing to-day. She refused to accept the result of scientific observations as they refuse to accept the result of religious knowledge and experience.

It is obvious that no conscientious student of nature and man can accept a "truth which cannot be proved," and make such a truth the basis of his enquiries. He frequently makes hypotheses which are not strictly-speaking based on fact, but he must verify these suppositions before attaching any positive value to them. There is no such thing as a scientific dogma, because the moment any physical or human knowledge becomes dogmatic, it ceases to be scientific. Even such a universally accepted theory as the Newtonian theory is not final because, the moment new facts are observed which do not fit into this theory, it must be modified or replaced by another, such as relativity. We cannot deny the result of direct observations, but the conclusions drawn from them may be altered by further observations made through more powerful instruments or due to the opening of a new field of investigation. That is why the conception of progress, so wrongly applied to human development, may safely be applied to scientific development. The discovery that the earth was not flat but round was a progress, the further possible discovery that it is of a shape slightly different from the one ascribed to it to-day would be another distinct progress. It is in the nature of human knowledge based on the observation of the outside world to change in time and space, just as it is in the nature of religion based on divine revelation of the spiritual world to establish its foundation on absolute truth which neither space, nor time, nor human observation can possibly alter.

To put it in other words, if religion is belief in God, religion implies acceptance of the dogmas revealed by God. If we say that God came on earth as Christ and taught us to believe certain things, we can discuss the respective accuracy of the records which have reached us of His teaching, but we cannot possibly question the teaching itself because, if we did, we should cease to believe either in the Incarnation or in God. The acceptance of a dogma by the Christian is just as unavoidable as its rejection by the atheist. The latter is perfectly consistent, for unbelief implies the limitation of man's knowledge to a certain aspect of the world, and excludes necessarily any truth of an absolute and eternal character, and more particularly any truth which cannot be tested by criticism and experiment. If the atheist accepted a dogma, he would indeed abdicate his freedom, because he would admit that a purely human truth is never subjected to change. That admission would not only be irrational, it would paralyse scientific progress. Every temporary hypothesis would become an eternal law.

Trained in this attitude of mind, the unbeliever, whether agnostic or materialist, cannot understand that the Christian should be ready to accept a dogma and to believe in what he cannot prove more firmly than any man can believe in what he can prove. Everything depends on the nature of the dogma. If you refuse to question a truth which can be proved, you limit your freedom, but if you refuse to question a truth which is beyond proof and even reason, you remain consistent and your freedom is not impaired. The mediaevalist said: *"Credo quia absurdum."* In his *Androcles and the Lion*, Shaw puts the same decisive argument in the mouth of his Christian martyr: "If I could understand my faith, it would no longer be worth dying for."

God cannot be the subject of human knowledge. He can neither be observed nor analysed. If you accept Him, you accept the essential principles of His teaching and may, through His grace, succeed in applying them to the conditions in which you are living. If you reject Him, you reject all revealed dogmas, but you refuse at the same time to devote your attention to the consideration of the most fundamental questions which explain human destiny and determine human conduct. In order to preserve your intellectual freedom in a field where it can only exercise itself within strict limits, you renounce the faculty of discovering through revelation the aim and scope of your own life and the fundamental principles of individual and social morality. For there is no such thing as an atheistic or sceptical morality.

This does not imply that all unbelievers are immoral, still less than all believers are morally sound. It merely implies that the latter have a chance of becoming so, because they have been given the rules of the game, while the first, whatever their personal qualities, confess through their refusal to accept these rules that their playing must necessarily be somewhat erratic. As long as the atheists retain the moral instincts inherited from a Christian education, they remain morally sound in spite of their philosophy of life. When they lose these instincts, they can only depend either on conventions deprived of authority, or on a human law dictated by changing circumstances in which good and evil are determined by material success or failure, prosperity or want. This attitude leads inevitably to individual, national or racial selfishness.

The tragedy of modern times is the tragedy of a man who denies the existence of the stars because he is short-sighted, or more exactly of a man who abdicates the freedom of comprehending God because he insists on preserving the freedom of comprehending the universe according to his limited power, without divine help. His limited knowledge does not provide him with any guidance. He is free, of course, to go anywhere, but he does not know where to go. Even if he did, he would lose his bearings. He wanders aimlessly in an intellectual black-out, knocking himself against every obstacle. And since there are millions of his fellow-men wandering in opposite directions, there is at least a probability that he will quarrel with some of them.

.   .   .   .   .

This picture only applies to individual cases. What happens in history, in a godless world, is somewhat different.

The necessity of asserting an absolute truth is so deep-rooted and so compelling that in order to achieve unity of purpose and escape from chaos, man-made dogmas must be substituted for revealed dogmas. These human catch-words are sooner or later found defective, but meanwhile they are likely to cause endless trouble. For if divine principles, owing to man's inability to interpret them rightly, do not lead straight to the Kingdom of God, human principles which are defective by nature and origin and which suffer therefore from a great deal more misinterpretation, are not likely to be more helpful.

The cry of Madame Roland, on her way to the guillotine still resounds in our ears; *"Liberté, que de crimes on commet en ton nom!"* If Madame Roland had spoken in the future tense, her words would be considered to-day as a true prophecy. What crimes have not been perpetrated in the name of Freedom? What crimes will not be committed in her name in the future? For it is a sad omen that the only dogma on which this undogmatic world seems to agree in its fight against autocracy is this man-made dogma of Liberty. Is is because, by accepting everything but unlimited political tyranny, it accepts in fact the most varied solutions of our economic and moral problems, from Communism to Capitalism, and from the rejection of all morality to the admission and combination of all moralities?

Christians have never believed in the secular gospel of the French Revolution and are not likely to believe in any new form which may be given it in the future. For the liberty of the Christian is the liberty of rejecting temptation and devoting himself to the service of God. His will is free because God made it so. His will is free in order that he should choose the right way for the sake of God. His will is free so that he might love God freely, God and his neighbour, his wife, his children, his friends, his fellow-men all over the world. When the Christian has exercised his freedom in these various ways, in worship, prayer and action, when he has discharged to the best of his ability his material and moral responsibilities, he discovers that he has not a moment left to think of his own life and of the "fulfilment of his personality." It is quite possible that his vocation as a man may coincide with his vocation as a Christian, but viewed in the Christian perspective, his personality is reduced to very small proportions. So is freedom estimated in human terms.

There is only one vocation, the vocation to serve God

and man. There is only one fulfilment, the fulfilment of the love of God. There is only one freedom, the freedom to sacrifice freedom. There is only one liberty, the liberty of the children of God in the Kingdom of God.

The gift of freedom is the most dangerous gift God made to man, because it allowed man to misuse all his other gifts, his senses and mind and his power over nature. It is the condition of honour, dignity, personality, but it is also the means of losing them. The whole conception of life and freedom has been turned upside down by the humanist. He assumed that man's power would gradually replace the power formerly attributed to God. Man's stature has never been so small and man's power has never been so misused. Is it not time that the unbeliever should ask himself whether there may not be a shadow of truth in the old "legend" according to which the quality of the relationship between man and man depends on the relationship between man and God, and the wise exercise of human freedom on the recognition of the divine love which granted this freedom?

IV.

MEDIAEVALISM AND HUMANISM

I

ONE OF THE MAIN MISTAKES OF OUR MODERN EDUCATION IS
that it neglects the Christian tradition on which our
civilisation is based. When I left school, I was under the
impression that the history of Europe was divided into two
main periods, the classical period illustrated by the art
and literature of Athens, and Rome, and the modern
period, including the story of Spain, France, England and
Germany, and of their struggles to dominate Europe.
Between the two periods was an era of barbarism, the
Middle Ages, which was distinguishable by its feudal
castles and monasteries, brutality and superstition, a dark
night separating the golden days of classical and modern
culture. Having heard nothing of the first centuries of
Christianity and very little of the intellectual and economic development of Europe before the Renaissance, I
was under the impression that the downfall of the Roman
Empire had left a gap in the world which had only been
filled ten centuries later, and that, instead of being the
main influence which had preserved culture, and later
brought it to a supreme development, the Church had
been responsible for this prolonged eclipse.

Instead of dispelling this strange error, my university
education at Brussels confirmed it. This was not only due
to personal ignorance, but also to the prejudice of my
teachers and of the authors whose books they gave me to
read. For Liberalism and Socialism were not only political or economic theories, they possessed their own in-

71

terpretation of history and literature, which was biased against any social or intellectual activity even remotely connected with religion in general, and the Roman Catholic Church in particular. Enlightened tolerance was indeed the privilage of the few, both in anti-clerical and in Catholic circles, and I was not fortunate enough to meet it.

The heroes I worshipped, in those days, were Michelangelo, Rabelais and Shakespeare. After looking through the latter's works in a bad French translation discovered in my mother's library, I decided to read him in the original and studied English for that purpose. I had preserved valuable memories of the Greek authors I had read at school, specially of Homer, but I found in the Renaissance a wealth of colour, a display of verbal riches which dazzled me and left me dumb with admiration. I not only read Shakespeare; I studied him through Brandes and Edward Dowden. I still have on my shelves *Shakespeare—His Mind and Art*, published in 1901, in which I underlined the following passage:

"In the Renaissance and Reformation period life had grown a real thing—this life on earth for three score years and ten. The terror and sadness of the Middle Ages, the abandonment of earthly joy, the wistfulness and pathos of spiritual desire, and on the other hand the scepticism, irony and sensuality under the ban were things which, as dominant forms of human life, had passed away."

No self-respecting scholar would express such views to-day, but most nineteenth century critics were either ignorant or colour-blind, as far as the Middle Ages were concerned. A somewhat naive young student might have been excused for accepting such opinions when they were expounded with so much eloquence by writers of great reputation.

. . . . .

I envy people who are able to quote the date of their conversion and to float, so to speak, "on the wings of

Hope to the heaven of Faith," like birds escaping from the cage of unbelief. Not being so favoured, I visualize my youth as a long struggle during which I spent most of my energies in removing the obstacles in my way, and as a series of accidents which occurred to me as soon as I attempted to fly.

It was indeed a roundabout journey and it would be difficult to give a connected account of its various stages. There are nevertheless certain landmarks which remain fixed in my mind to this day.

In spite of my intellectual arrogance, I was not so foolish as to believe that the sketch of history which had been presented to me was not comprehensive, and I seized every opportunity of completing it. This led me to devote my leisure—I was by then earning a modest living as a part-time teacher—to the reading of French mediaeval literature. I devoured a number of mystery plays, epics, romances and ballads which soon made me realize—as the most superficial knowledge of Chaucer might have brought Dowden to realize—that the Middle Ages were not so black as they were painted, and that the master-pieces of the Renaissance which I so much admired were deeply rooted in mediaevalism. The eclipse of which I had heard so much had already passed by the time the first cathedrals reared their towers to the sky of France, and when trade and industry transformed the towns of Italy and Flanders into beehives of activity. The "gap" between classical and modern cultures had been bridged by that Church which was supposed to have created it; from the beginning to the end of the transition period, the monasteries had preserved order and learning in a world torn asunder by disorder and ignorance. I found that my teachers' generalisations had been somewhat hasty and that the Christian tradition had never been entirely broken, from its origin to its apparent decadence.

The fact that this decadence coincided with the Renaissance, with the "rebirth of a dead civilisation," upset the scheme of history which I had hitherto accepted.

My reading of the mystics, prompted by my admiration for Maeterlinck's first book of essays, *Le Trésor des Humbles*, convinced me that if Ruysbroeck, Eckhart or Boehme were labouring under illusions, these illusions were not devoid of a certain austere beauty, and I had a hard struggle in reconciling my shaken atheism to the attraction I began to feel for the spiritual life. True, I still dabbled in these subjects as a mere dilettante and looked upon them as poetic creations, but it dawned on me that such poetry might have at least as much foundation in reality as the romantic lyrics which had stirred my enthusiasm a few years before. If the love of God was a beautiful dream, the love of man and woman exalted in these lyrics might also be a dream. Where could I draw the line between illusion and reality?

These doubts coincided with my first disappointment in love. I call it this in the perspective of a long life, but it was at the time a heart-breaking experience. A sky-rocket is not a star, but you may burn your fingers if you handle it carelessly. It is characteristic of my romantic state of mind that I escaped to Italy in the hope of finding some salve for my wound, and still more characteristic that I found it there so soon. Although I would not have admitted it at the time, my first visit to Tuscany showed me that my tragedy was not so final as I had imagined, and that I had not lost all interest in life. Had I been a pure romantic, I would have filled the notebooks I carried in my knapsack with poems expressing my despair; I filled them instead with notes on mediaeval frescoes and sculptures. I should have felt and said that the past had lost its glory; I felt instead that a new world was suddenly revealed to me and that every step of my journey led to fresh discoveries, that I was brought at last face to face with an art so sincere and direct that it surpassed the most stirring modern poem or picture.

Faithful to my habit of travelling light, I had only taken three books with me: Burckhardt's *Cicerone*, the Franciscan *Legend of the Three Companions* and a translation of Dante's *Divina Commedia*. I also picked up in a library on my way a small guide book called *The Mornings in Florence*, by a certain John Ruskin, whose name had been mentioned to me a few months before. This was the second landmark on my journey.

I know the smile which the name of Ruskin provokes to-day in artistic circles, but I am not ashamed to acknowledge my debt to this erratic and impulsive prophet. We are apt to forget that, with Carlyle, he did more than any other writer to reveal the Middle Ages to a Victorian England, basking in self-satisfaction, "enlightenment and progress." He restored the balance of history by reinterpreting the lesson taught by the carvings of the French cathedrals and the paintings of Giotto and his school. He warned the industrialists that they were leading the world to certain destruction. He had the outstanding merit of giving the lie to the pleasant appearances which deceived most of his contemporaries, and of revealing the value of a past too long forgotten or too hastily dismissed. A French critic called him *un sourcier*, a discoverer of hidden springs, and his works remain as a record of the discovery of Mediaevalism. He stands as the forerunner of a movement which is gathering force to-day and which may still bring Christian culture into the channel of world civilisation.

I decided there and then to translate *The Mornings* into French, to complete the guide book and bring it up to date. Before I had finished my work, the small pamphlet had grown into a ponderous volume which was followed by several others. Within a few years, Ruskin's ideas became accessible to the French public,[1] and I had incidentally begun my training as a writer, for there is no better training for a beginner than the stern discipline of translation.

After this, every summer holiday was spent in Italy. With a faithful friend who shared my enthusiasm for what is so wrongly called the art of the "primitives," I walked through Lombardy, Tuscany and Umbria, searching out any mediaeval monument or painting. The names of Padua and Giotto, Castiglione and Masolino, Siena and Duccio, Florence and Angelico, Arezzo and Piero, and a score of other places, Pisa and her Campo Santo, San Gimignano and her "beautiful towers," and above all Assisi, with the two churches of San Francesco, still ring in my ears like the peal of Florentine bells heard in the evening from the Piazza Michelangelo.

We crossed the Pisan hills between Lucca and Pisa, and scaled the Apennines up to the Camaldoli, whence both the Mediterranean and the Adriatic can be seen glittering in the sun. We made a pilgrimage from Assisi to the stern mountain of La Verna, where St. Francis received the Holy Stigmata. We walked through austere and smiling landscapes, barren hills dressed in brown Franciscan habits, rows of prophetic cypresses standing like huge candlesticks in the burning sun, and vineyards and olive groves shaded with poplars. We imagined ourselves to be pilgrims visiting the shrine of civilisation. We looked down upon the valleys of the Po and the Arno, as travellers who had reached the Holy Land.

Nature had been my first worship. In those days I wor-

---

[1] I alone was not responsible for this. Marcel Proust published *La Bible d'Amiens,* and other translations, almost at the same time.

shipped both Nature and Art. I was not consciously worshipping God, but I realized that artistic creations dedicated to the greater glory of God and inspired by a popular religion, possess spiritual qualities which no technical power or individual genius can give to post-Renaissance works. I began to ask myself whether these qualities did not flow from a mysterious source which was more intimately related to my being than the most brilliant achievements I had hitherto admired. I asked myself this question: "Why did Faith give such power to man?"

. . . . . .

It is with no feeling of pride that I have taken such trouble to record the various stages of my journey towards Christianity. It is painful to have to admit that this journey was slow and halting, obstructed by prejudice, self-consciousness and intellectual pride. Any child, brought up in Christian surroundings, was closer to God than I was as I grew up. In spite of the fact that I had enjoyed all the advantages of a "good education" and that I had been fortunate enough to widen my knowledge by reading and travelling, I was still deciphering the alphabet of Christianity while others were already able to read and even to pray. I was like a traveller who, after losing his way in a wild country, is compelled to retrace his steps. There was no short cut possible. I had to pay for every mistake I had made since my childhood. Even the value of truthfulness which had been so deeply impressed upon me, stood in my way. I was afraid of being carried away by sentiment, and of professing a belief prompted by a wish to believe, rather than by "real conviction."

There is no doubt that my appreciation of religious art, literature and music had brought me nearer to Christianity than my vague nature worship. It is less dangerous to look for God in divinely inspired works than in a beautiful but disordered creation. But it is better still to allow the grace of God to take hold of us, independent of any intellectual truth or artistic beauty. Such truth and beauty only confirm our faith, they are not the source of it.

The root of the trouble, in the conversion of an agnostic, is that he appreciates everything according to the pleasure he derives from it. The most ideal selflessness, the sincere craving for the noblest thoughts and impressions is still self-centred. The most ignorant or naive faith is God-centred. It implies complete surrender, and complete surrender is the last state of mind which a secularly educated person would dream of reaching.

Faith does not usually come to us through human truth or beauty; it comes to us as the renunciation of all that we call beautiful and true for the love of God.

II

When we visualize the Middle Ages, we think of an age in complete contrast with the modern world. Before the sixteenth century the economic activity of Western Europe was almost entirely agricultural. Industry was in the hands of craftsmen organized in close corporations. Trade remained the monopoly of groups of merchants who practised barter or used elementary methods of credit. The serfs or small farmers who tilled the fields depended on their landlords for their military security, as the traders depended on the princes for the safety of the roads. The whole framework of society was a close organisation in which individual freedom was subordinated to political and religious authority. The Church held in her strong hands all the threads of religious and intellectual activity. She organized the schools and universities, and safeguarded, not only the spiritual, but also the temporal law. She inspired the works of architects, sculptors, painters and poets. She claimed St. Peter's keys to the gates of Heaven and, for the majority, this was the goal of human life. Many people, no doubt, ignored her advice or openly criticized some of her practices, but these gibes were mainly directed against the clergy, not against their doctrine or faith. The main theme of mediaeval satire was the contrast between the behaviour of certain priests and the Gospel which they preached. Such attacks did not shake the strong foundations on which mediaeval life was built. They sprang in many cases from religious zeal and not from lack of faith. There was a protestant element in Catholicism before the Reformation, which, on several occasions, notably in the thirteenth century, through the activity of the Franciscan and Dominican orders, reformed the Church from inside.

In every department of human activity, Mediaevalism shows man in a state of complete subordination. God crowns the picture and all men, great and small, are under His authority. The Church and even the State (since the Head of the State held his power from God) derived their right to govern the people from the same divine source. Authority permeated the whole social body but, if it was abused, there was always the possibility of appealing against the temporal power to the spiritual. Christ remained the supreme judge on earth and in heaven. He separated the sheep from the goats. His Last Judgment, painted and carved in every Church, was at the same time the comfort of the oppressed and the terror of the oppressor. The hope of the good man was salvation; the fear of the bad man, damnation. These ideas prevailed in every class of society, in every country. Nations were only a group of towns and principalities loosely knit together. If social life was centred around the feudal castle or the clock-tower, religion spread from one country to another through the Church, by means of one language (Latin), one worship, one liturgy, one culture inspired by one faith. The Cross broke all national barriers.[2]

The Middle Ages may be considered as an attempt to curb man's sinfulness through discipline and to lead him to redemption through worship and work. This is not the place to discuss how far this attempt succeeded. It is enough to point out that, before the sixteenth century, the emphasis in Western civilisation was on God and His purpose for man. The fact that many mediaeval practices were contrary to the most elementary principles of Christianity does not affect this conclusion.

. . . .

The gradual decadence of Mediaevalism coincides with the rise of Humanism. This term is used to-day to describe the ideas, popular in the nineteenth century, which were based on Jean Jacques Rousseau's views of nature and man. Fifty years ago, it applied only to the culture favoured at the time of the Renaissance, and inspired by the study of classical philosophy. Apparently sixteenth and nineteenth century Humanism are in strong contrast to each other. The first merely endeavours to restore man to his proper place in the universe, without challenging the Christian faith. The second discards all Church discipline, claims man's right to organize society for the sole purpose of satisfying his instincts and aspirations, and substitutes for revealed religion either agnosticism

---

[2] Cf H. W. C. Davis (*Mediaeval Europe*, p. 154): "What appeals to us in the mediaeval outlook is first the idea of mankind as a brotherhood transcending racial and political divisions . . . ; secondly, a profound belief in the superiority of right over might, of spirit over matter, of the eternal interests of humanity over the ambitions and pursuits of the passing hour."

or a vague theism leading to the worship of human reason. The later development of Humanism is nevertheless the natural consequence of the earlier one. There have been in the past, and there may still be in the future, many compromises between the mediaeval and the modern conceptions of human life, but any balance between the two tendencies has become impossible. The centre of gravity must shift either one way or the other, towards the worship of Man and the secularisation of religion, or towards the worship of God and the spreading of the Gospel among men. The Renaissance is merely the beginning of a movement which found its full expression in the French Revolution and in the era of Liberalism which followed it.

In some countries, the period of transition between Mediaevalism and Humanism lasted longer than in others; but, whether slowly or rapidly, peacefully or violently, Western civilisation in all its aspects underwent a complete transformation. The problems of death and suffering were evaded. Sin was denied, because its existence was not consistent with the doctrine of the goodness of nature and man. The main purpose of law was said to be the preservation of human liberties and the defence of civic rights. Free trade and free competition took the place of economic control. The ambition of the individual dominated the interest of the community in the same way as national ambition dominated international relations. Religion was treated as a decaying tradition in Roman Catholic countries or as an idealistic aspiration in Protestant countries.

Other causes hastened and favoured the movement, such as scientific discoveries and industrial developments. These achievements encouraged the opinion that since the natural world contained no secret which could not be brought to light, the problem of human destiny which had always been considered as a religious question, would be as elegantly solved some day as any scientific problem. There was no limit to progress and progress meant more knowledge, more education, more discoveries, more production, more trade and greater individual enterprise in industry. "The Kingdom, the power and the glory" passed from God to man. Humility was scorned and pride exalted, pride in the human race, in its efficiency, strength and reason; and the rock of Christianity trembled in an earthquake of doubt, atheism, and revolt.

There came a time, at the end of the last century, when abstract thought was strongly discouraged and when the positivist teaching of Herbert Spencer and Auguste Comte was offered to European university students as the pattern of modern wisdom. Some of those who had discarded the Christian revelation still insisted on exploring the realm of metaphysics, in a vain endeavour to discover in Descartes, Kant and their followers some meaning in life. They were told that such preoccupations could lead nowhere since they were beyond the scope of human intelligence, which was only concerned with the relation between the subject and the object. There could not be such a thing as positive reality and to seek for it was a sheer waste of time. The only reality was the relationship existing between the self and the external world, and it was on this relationship that attention should be centred. Every effort was made to exclude from the field of human enquiry problems such as the origin of the world, the purpose of life, the reason for pain and death, which did not fit into the new determinist scheme. Ethics were reduced to the formula: "the greatest good of the greatest number," and the freedom of the individual was only limited by the duty of respecting the freedom of his neighbours.

The prevailing idea was that the kingdom of God occupied on the map of human knowledge and wisdom the same place as *terra incognita* on the map of the world, and that, as the space allowed for undiscovered lands became more and more restricted by fresh discoveries, this imaginary realm would find its place among the relics of an ignorant past. Human progress would burst the bubble of religion. Fear which had been used and abused by the Church would no longer bolster up her prestige. With the help of popular scientists, rationalists were prepared to find reasons for everything and to sweep the cobwebs of legend from the sky. Man triumphant had, through his own power and intelligence, set his feet on the road, and would not stop until he had reached his goal, unhampered and unaided by any supernatural agent. He would henceforth be captain of his soul, master of his fate: *"Excelsior," "Ad Astra."*[3]

. . . . .

The contrast between Humanism and Mediaevalism does not involve any definite judgment of these two periods of Western civilisation. Like all human developments they contain good and evil. Both claim outstanding heroes who lived and died for their ideals or for their faith; both have left behind them monuments of intellectual and artistic genius which enrich our tradition. From the scientific point of view, the comparison is all in favour of Humanism. From the point of view of art, music and literature, the modern period did not, it is true, produce a united body of culture comparable to that which gave expression to the Christian faith in

[3] This sketch of the spirit of the modern period may appear exaggerated to the English and American readers, because they have never so clearly recognized the opposition between Humanism and Mediaevalism as on the Continent. We are concerned, however, not with England and America alone, but with Western Europe in which first France and later Germany exerted a predominating influence.

Western Europe in the thirteenth and fourteenth centuries, but it gave to the world a number of painters, composers and poets whose individual power stands unequalled. The very tension which arose from the great illusion fostered by the worship of Man, and the inevitable disillusions which followed, gave birth to the music of Mozart, Beethoven and Brahms, the art of Michelangelo, Rubens and Turner, the poetry of Goethe, Keats and Browning.

If the appreciation of a period of history depended on its intellectual achievements, it would be difficult to decide whether mankind lost more than it gained when it left the shelter of the Church to wander through the smiling valley of Classicism or to scale the wild mountains of Romanticism. It is only when we consider the moral and religious aspects of the period that Humanism fills us with doubt and dismay. It has its heroes, but it is not heroic; it has its martyrs, but it is not holy; it seeks unity but finds confusion. We watch its efforts as we might watch the struggle of some wild beast caught in a trap.

The sure symptom of this unrest is an increasing cruelty in warfare. There had been armed conflicts on a limited scale in the Middle Ages, but from the sixteenth century we witness an almost uninterrupted succession of wars in Europe, between England and Spain, France and the Empire, France and England, the monarchies and the French Republic, the Coalition and Napoleon, Russia and the Western Powers, Prussia and France, the Triple Alliance and the Triple Entente, the Axis and the United Nations, a rising tide of violence and brutality involving larger and larger armies, more and more destructive weapons, and ending by engulfing civilians and soldiers, women and children, and inflicting upon them all the horrors of air bombardment and famine, until the last sign of love and pity seems to have disappeared from the world.

The most astonishing feature of this destructive spirit in the domain of reality is that it runs parallel with a constructive spirit in the domain of ideals. The "Brotherhood of Man" is followed by the Napoleonic wars, the "Holy Alliance" by Power Politics, International Socialism by National Socialism, the Hague Conventions by 1914, the League of Nations by 1939. The greater the demand, the greater the catastrophe which follows the demand; the higher the hope, the deeper the despair.

This is the problem which confronts us to-day. How is it that when men clamour louder and louder for security and peace, they can only obtain terror and war? To question the sincerity of the hope is no honest answer, for the hope is not only inspired by generous feelings, but also by the obvious interest of the vast majority. Neither is it sound history to place all the responsibility on some nation or group of nations whose warlike spirit has been the immediate cause of the present conflict. We are faced with the results of a gradual disintegration which started four centuries ago, and the events which we are witnessing to-day cannot be understood if we do not trace their origin to the time when this disintegration began.

Humanism must be considered as a whole. In this light, it appears as a bold experiment which went wrong.

. . . . . .

Against this stormy background of clouds and lightning, a few cathedrals are still seen standing in our cities as the last relics of a time in which man's violence, cruelty, greed and perfidy were often evident, but in which these evils were at least acknowledged and in which people lived and strove under one God, in one Faith.

At the present turning point of history, it seems more urgent than ever to enquire why the humanist experiment went wrong, why so many generous efforts failed and why the love of mankind ended in conflict and hatred. Who bears the responsibility? The governors or the governed, the leaders or the people, the philosophers or their disciples? And if, as we believe, the responsibility is shared by all, should we not ask ourselves whether the trouble is not at the very root of the human tree, whether the experiment did not go wrong because it was wrong to make it? From the first to the fifteenth century Western civilisation grew stronger and stronger on the Christian formula of "God made Man." From the sixteenth century to the present day it has weakened more and more rapidly on the formula of "Man made God." During the Christian era, Christianity was faced by successive disruptions, such as the downfall of the Roman Empire, the invasion of the Barbarians and the petty quarrels of feudalism. It was a slow, halting progress, at a time when progress was never mentioned, towards a wiser love, a nobler culture, a greater unity. The pride derived from these achievements was partly responsible for the reaction which followed and which placed Man, not God, in the centre of the universe. At that moment, as Chesterton pointed out, man "took the wrong turning." He followed a road which led him to disaster, in spite of all the advantages he derived from a learning much wider than that of his forefathers, and from discoveries which they never dreamt of. Every victory was turned into defeat. Colonisation was followed by slavery, industrialism by the exploitation of the workers or unemployment, science by the last refinement in the art of warfare. Every weapon man forged for himself and which was supposed to subject the blind forces of nature to his will was twisted in his hands and turned against himself. Humanism progressed from the point of view of scientific knowledge, trade activity, industrial equipment, but it failed to use such progress for the benefit of the race. It lost on the moral and religious side what it gained on the material side.

Once more we are bound to ask ourselves whether the worship of man is not the fundamental cause of this failure. Some people say that man has gone mad. They are literally right. Self-worship always ends in madness.

. . . . . .

The failure of Humanism has already been recognized by the leaders of religious and philosophical thought. Unless it is recognized by the people, there is no hope of cutting loose from the vicious circle of illusions and disillusions, utopias and catastrophes in which it has involved mankind. The experiment stands condemned not because it is ignoble or corrupt, but because it is mistaken and opposed to man's true nature and to his relation to God and the universe. It is the most grievous error ever made, and the fact that it was made in some instances for disinterested motives makes it all the more pitiable.

There is a radical difference between a sound doctrine which is either misinterpreted or exploited by man's sinfulness, and an unsound doctrine which leads to disaster through its very unsoundness. In the first case, there is always a chance of recovery because the doctrine may be reasserted and the mistakes corrected. In the second case, there is no chance of recovery because the more insistently and sincerely the unsound doctrine is reasserted, the more disastrous will be the consequences. It may be rightly contended that Mediaevalism fell into disrepute through the abuses prevalent throughout Europe in the fifteenth and sixteenth centuries, and that some radical changes had become necessary. The tragedy is that the humanists, instead of altering the structure of the edifice, ended by destroying it to its foundations.

When people argue that "you cannot set back the clock," they mean either that the new order which they hope to build in the twentieth century cannot be the same as the old order which prevailed in the thirteenth and fourteenth, or that the principles of Humanism are unalterable. They frequently add that progress being continuous, the new order must necessarily develop on the same lines as the order which preceded it, and can have nothing in common with a more distant period.

These statements reveal an extraordinary confusion of thought. The idea of an inevitable improvement in human civilisation can no longer be accepted. Progress has been destroyed by its inventors more efficiently than by its staunchest opponents. Neither does the idea of a smooth and gradual evolution stand the test of experience. We live in the midst of catastrophes and they are not the first which have disrupted the course of history since the days of Egypt and Nineveh. The past is not dead. Social and individual life is repeatedly interrupted by switchbacks and revivals. The Renaissance is itself a return to the art and ideas of a remote period, far more distant from the fifteenth century than the fifteenth century is from us. All that can be said on this subject is that, if the spirit of a former age may be recovered, the forms which it will take in the new age will be different. The mistake made by the early defenders of Mediaevalism, like Ruskin, was that, instead of insisting on the spirit, they insisted on the form. Nothing is "impossible," but some things are not practicable, and the hope of feeding a densely populated country, in which agriculture had been neglected for a long time, on the income derived from village industries run on William Morris' lines, was rightly considered utopian. It is foolish to make the fatalistic assumption that because some economic or political development has followed certain lines in the immediate past, it is bound to follow the same lines in the future; it is as foolish to declare that a complete transformation of society will take place because a few writers and artists refuse to accept the mediocrity and vulgarity of the modern world. There are certain things in human life which are more important than the fastidiousness of artistic refinement. The problem is not to transform man's surroundings but to convert his soul. It is on the cardinal principles of Mediaevalism that we should take our stand, not on one or the other of its outward aspects. It is an inadequate defence of religion to say that it should be preserved because it inspired the Gregorian chant, the poetry of Dante and the builders of the great cathedrals. Christianity is the story of the redemption of man, through the Love of God, or it is nothing. It did not find its complete artistic expression before the late Middle Ages, and this expression could only take place because Christian forms and ideas had been cultivated and developed through a long spiritual struggle during which art and learning had stood in the background. The "Dark Ages" had to remain dark for a long time before the light of beauty dawned on the Church.

The fall of Humanism will not be brought about by the failures which have met attempts to build it or rebuild it on stronger foundations. Optimism dies hard, and it is always possible to explain every failure by circumstances which blind us to its true cause. Before the French Revolution, this cause was considered to be the abuse of the royal power and the privileges enjoyed by the aristocracy, and they were duly suppressed. Later, failure was attributed to the class distinction resulting from inequality of wealth and to trade rivalries between nations. To-day, the danger of autocracy and racial hatred is denounced from every pulpit and every platform. All these protests, although justified, do not reach the root of the trouble because they only attack one of the aspects of the fundamental evil which is man's pride and his separation from God. If we can base our hope on nothing but an improvement in social and international relations, there is no reason to think that mankind will not go on building up new systems and floundering into new catastrophes, because each of these systems only deals with one superficial result of the fundamental evil and ignores the evil itself which produces new crises leading to new disasters. If Communism and Federalism were to rule the world tomorrow, they would bring with them miseries similar to those which followed "the Rights of Man," Capitalism, Constitutionalism, or Fascism, because they would rest on the same fallacy that man had "the right" to be happy.

In spite of the fact that the doctrine of human goodness has been severely shaken and that people smile to-day whenever Rousseau's *"bon sauvage"* is mentioned, the belief in individual righteousness or in the righteousness of a certain system, class or nation still prevails. It is always the "other fellow" who is in the wrong, the "bourgeois" or the "demagogue," "Jerry" or the "decadent plutocrat." A thing is not said to be good or bad according to eternal standards revealed by God, but according to circumstances which may vary from month to month. Russia, who was denounced in the strongest terms when she made a pact with the enemy, is extolled the moment she becomes a valuable ally. A neutral abused because his neutrality appears, at a certain moment, to hamper our war effort, is treated with respect and praised for his wisdom when this same neutrality relieves us from strategic anxieties. Our society is riddled with inconsistencies which are the direct result of our selfishness. There is no end to the compromises we are prepared to make when our interests are at stake. This is not to say that our judgments are always wrong. The rightness or wrongness of our judgments are not so much concerned here as the reasons which prompt us to make them. If we do not know what is right and what is wrong, how are we to determine any responsibility, whether it be our own or that of another and, what is still more important, where are we to draw the line between the two? Humanism provides only one answer: "Man follows the dictates of his conscience," which really means that each man decides for himself what he must do or think. For the dictates of conscience are not the same for every individual or nation, nor do they remain the same for every individual or nation.

These actions and reactions are inevitable as long as we do not recognize that there is no stable order apart from God, since God is the only authority to which man can submit himself without losing his freedom. As long as this supernatural and therefore supernational authority is not acknowledged, man will go on fighting in order to conquer or to recover his self-righteous illusions.

. . . .

The great efforts made during the last centuries to establish a permanent order based on Law should not be ignored. The Rule of Law was emphasized by Liberalism. The more liberal the institutions of a country or the relationship between countries, the more it was found necessary to reinforce the national and international structure by a framework of constitutions and treaties preserving those concerned from the abuse of force. But Law is not an end in itself, it merely legalizes decisions taken by the State, whether the authority in power is legitimate or not. It cannot enforce its decisions apart from this authority and is merely used by it as a means to an end.

National law may establish a democratic or autocratic regime; it may even for a time restrict the use of popular liberty or, in certain circumstances, the abuse of the Executive, but its quality will always depend on the quality of the political regime which it serves. International law may prevent aggression or intimidation as long as the States which wield the greatest military or economic power agree to support it, and they will only agree if they are satisfied with the position they occupy. Ultimately, the prestige of treaties rests on the potential use of force, on the efficiency of the punishment of the law-breaker. Any confidence placed in the judicial power, apart from the executive power on which it rests, must bring about disaster; just as blind faith in any man-made system has always ended, and must always end, in failure. A strongly armed Law can restrain the weak, but an unarmed human law can never restrain the strong.

. . . .

Both Humanism and Christianity are strongly criticized to-day, the first because evil in man's nature has become so blatant that no one can any longer deny its existence, the second because those who have pursued the wildest dreams still refuse to accept the truths revealed in the Gospel. But there is this fundamental difference. The humanistic ideal has been tried again and again and has led us into deeper and deeper despair. "The Christian ideal," as Chesterton remarked, "has not been tried and found wanting; it has been found difficult, and left untried." Humanism is contrary to the laws of nature, Christianity is not bound by them. The old Humanism has reached its twilight, the Christian renaissance has not yet reached its dawn.

The complete fall of Humanism will not be brought about by the failure of its political systems or ethical methods. For although these failures reveal the cardinal error made from the moment that the centre of the universe was shifted from God to Man, this mistake may be renewed *ad infinitum* in the hope that the circumstances of to-morrow may be more favourable than those of yesterday. Society is not moved by sound reasoning; it is moved by sentiment, and as long as there is any hope that success may be achieved by following the same direction as before, there is little chance that this direction will be altered. The hope that, through his intellectual power and through his own resources, man might fulfil his destiny, was a very strong and, in some ways, a very noble one. This sentiment will be hard to kill and it can only be killed by another sentiment, more direct and burning, the sharp, tearing stab of pain.

Although the horrors of modern war surpass in scope and intensity the torments and cruelties brought about by earlier armed conflicts, although the tidal wave of famine and disease which swept over Europe during the first World War and the years which followed is once more making more victims than the worst plagues recorded in history, physical suffering alone will not bring about the conversion of the world. This conversion must be spiritual; only spiritual suffering caused by doubt, frustration, and the recurring torture of disillusionment will lead the majority of men to seek in God the centre of their existence and the goal of their efforts.

Humanistic hope will be killed by human despair.

V.

LIBERALISM AND CHRISTIANITY

I

IN SPITE OF THE ENTHUSIASM AROUSED BY MY FIRST VISITS TO Italy I remained at heart a pleasure seeker. The fact that the pleasures I sought were not of the kind which would have satisfied a coarse sensualist does not alter this disagreeable fact. I was once more living under my mother's roof and spent my free time in working with her. We translated the "Mornings" together and, as she knew Italian, she taught me to read Dante. I can still hear her husky voice scanning some lines from the *Inferno* and the *Purgatorio*—something interrupted us before we reached the *Paradiso*. I remember the armchair in which she sat in a shady corner of our small garden, her keen pale face framed in a halo of thin red hair, and the impatience she showed when I struggled too long over the notes of various commentators who did not always agree: "Oh! Leave your notes alone," she exclaimed, "can't you *hear*?"

She had been severely ill, and nursing her back to life had helped me to overcome the worst pangs of my old grief. It was a fine summer and we worked together for weeks, trying to unravel the skein of Dante's symbolism. She thought herself, a free-thinker and I already fancied myself as a Christian, but I feel sure that, at that time, she was closer to Christianity than I was. "I don't believe a word of all this," she exclaimed one day, "but if I did I should walk straight into a convent or start a revolution."

94

I believed, or thought I believed, a good deal, but I stayed beside her, in that quiet garden, listening to a blackbird perched on a poplar nearby.

I wonder sometimes why so many people shiver on the brink of faith without taking their lives into their hands and leaping into the stream. Is it faint-heartedness, false pride, or mere procrastination? Or do they find a certain pleasure in doubt, which prompts them to revive it before it disappears again?

The main difficulty is to join the Church. I felt that this decision was as binding as marriage, and while I should have had no hesitation in marrying any girl with whom I thought myself in love, I was afraid to take the final step, as far as my religion was concerned.

This was not so inconsistent as it appears on the surface. I suppose I felt that, in human affairs, I assumed my own responsibility, and would pay for the consequences if I blundered. I had already learnt that lesson to my own cost, and had emerged somewhat bruised but still very much alive from the ordeal. With regard to the Church, it was different. If I entered that door, I could never reopen it without leaving my soul behind. My life would be blighted and, in spite of what I said and wrote at the time, I cared desperately for my individual life and the joy of discovery.

From my secular education I had preserved strong suspicions of the organised Church and a blind confidence in my individual power. As long as I remained independent, I thought I would be free to act and write for the greater benefit of Christianity. I would even be in a better position to influence anti-clerical unbelievers. But if I joined the Church, my words would lose a great deal of their weight, and I might besides be unable to express myself freely, because I would be fettered by new loyalties. I looked upon the Church with a longing mixed with fear. It appeared to me, at the same time, as the sanctuary in which I wished to take refuge, and as the prison from which I could never escape.

If I am to tell the whole truth, I should add that one of the reasons which prevented me from joining the Church of Rome—I should remind the reader that I was still in Belgium—was founded on the reaction provoked by my fastidious tastes in religious art. Just as my Italian journeys had stirred my enthusiasm, the few attempts I made to attend services in Belgian churches stirred my antagonism. Modern churches are seldom attractive; the old Gothic churches which appealed so much to me were often desecrated by the wrong kind of decoration and restoration. The music was poor and the sermon still poorer. The finest cathedral is neither a museum nor a concert hall.

I am well aware that in calling such shortcomings blasphemous I was guilty of blasphemy. If I had had any experience of faith, I should have dropped on my knees after crossing the threshold of the most tawdry church, instead of looking round and venting my artistic indignation. I still had to learn that faith is not conditioned by artistic environments; but I have preserved some doubts to this day as to the necessity of looking at bad pictures, hearing bad music and erecting ugly buildings, when so much good music might be heard within whitewashed walls, under the noble rafters of a barn. If God is to be glorified by the works of man, should not these works be the best man can create? And if we are no longer able to create them should we not have the humility to admit it, instead of trying vainly to imitate the past?

There is no doubt a lack of sense of proportion in what Ruskin said on this subject, but we should beware of ignoring his advice. Just as the ardent faith of the Middle Ages is largely responsible for the Gothic Cathedral, so the sentimentality which stifles our modern faith is partly responsible for the religious imagery of our day. The gravest mistake Ruskin made was to imagine that the Pre-Raphaelites could solve the problem.

. . . . . .

I called, not long ago, on an old friend of mine whom I had not seen for years. We had both been severely battered by personal losses and, although we did not mention them, they were very much with us while we were talking of trivial things, such as the best way of making a madeira cake without madeira. Before we parted, I started to talk about the Church and its recent influence on my life. "Yes, I understand," he said, "I suppose I am a lonely bird. You see, I am not socially minded. I always feel unhappy in a crowd. . . ." I endeavoured to reassure him on this point; English and American churches are not usually overcrowded.

My friend, who incidentally is one of the greatest English writers living, is so much ahead of me in many ways that I may be forgiven if I compare his attitude to the one I adopted forty years ago. He is trying to live a Christian life without joining the Church of God, as I sincerely tried to be a Christian while retaining my independence and my fastidious sensitiveness.

I should paint a false picture of myself if I did not say here why I could not hold this perilous position, why I did not succeed in making a madeira cake without madeira. I failed because I attempted to make the best of two worlds which, as far as I am concerned, are incompatible. I tried to keep to a settled plan of religious readings and to say my prayers regularly. I fancied that these prayers might be heard and was overcome by waves of religious enthusiasm. I steeped myself in Christian art, Christian music, Christian poetry. I even attempted to translate these aspirations into action by helping others for the love of God, as I had helped them before for the sake of the social revolution. But all I succeeded in doing was to substitute for my former political convictions, for my nature-worship and mother-worship, a new worship essentially self-centred, which gave me an aim in life, but did not bring me much closer to God.

The truth of the matter is that I was still an individualist searching for happiness. I still believed implicitly, if not explicitly, that this happiness could only be realized in the expression of my own personality in family life and in individual religious life. It is only after thirty-five years of married life that I have begun to see the parable of the family, as the pattern of the Church, as well as of society.

True marriage is the subordination of self to the love of the family. True faith is the subordination, not only of self, but of all loyalties and allegiances, particularly that of the family, to the love of One God Almighty in His Church. No flower can grow in a garden overshadowed by trees. No guest can be made welcome if all the seats are taken round the fire. Surrender is the first condition of grace, as humility is the essential condition of worship.

I still had to learn that a prayer is as acceptable to God when it is said aloud in a motley crowd as when it is whispered in a bedroom, and that as long as I was presumptuous enough not to realize that I was in the same need of salvation as the most unattractive individual in that crowd, I was not in a fit state to pray.

.   .   .   .   .   .

I learnt it, like everything else, in a roundabout way. I learnt it from my wife.

If I were to enter here into the details of that remarkable story, it would throw this book out of balance. It began like a fairy tale and it ended in a piece of solid reality. We were divided in every way. She was English, I was Belgian; she had made a name on the stage; I was still an obscure teacher, with literary ambitions. She was a member of the Church, I stood outside; she lived in the world, as a Christian; I was only interested in the world in so far as it gave me what I asked. She believed in God and sacrificed herself; I, for my sins, had hitherto believed mostly in myself and had not yet realized what a poor belief it was. But this difference between Christian illusion and Christian reality did not confront us at first. When a rather bumptious young man of thirty goes to a recital for the purpose of writing a criticism for his paper, he is scarcely prepared to meet his fate. And when a young lady, after reciting some scenes from Shakespeare, reads the next day a glowing article on her performance, she does not jump to the rash conclusion that the author with a queer name is destined to be the companion of her life and the father of her six children.

I walked into this story like a poet who discovers his private muse; but I discovered much more than that. I discovered that my intolerance towards others was founded on a false notion of my own importance, that self-sacrifice matters more to love than the most eloquent passion, and that the only way to happiness is through the happiness of others. The secret of our relationship was and still is that, although I receive far more than I give, I retain the strange belief that I give as much as I receive. This is one of the last illusions I have preserved out of the thousand false illusions I have discarded. I wish to keep it as long as possible, because it stands as a mile-stone on the road of my life, as a monument of my past vanity.

I cannot tell what I may have taught my wife during

the last thirty-five years, but she certainly taught me the art of living. I do not use these words in the meaning generally given them, but in the meaning which should be given them. For the art of living does not consist of seeking pleasure, although pleasure should not be despised as such, but of seeking human and divine life. People should learn to live as they learn to swim, in order not to be afraid of taking risks, and to be able to throw themselves into their work and embark on every good enterprise without regard for the consequences. A bad swimmer makes a bad life-saver.

My wife never preached. She never asked me to go to church; but she went. . . . Although I would not dare to analyse her intentions, she led me exactly where she wanted to lead me, without mentioning the goal of our journey. I wished her to remain on the stage and my great ambition was to write plays for her. I never realized how incompatible these plans were with our wish to have a large family. She did, of course, but was wise enough not to disillusion me too soon. The result was that, instead of "giving full expression to our personalities" and displaying our talents to the world, we lived a hard and full life, absorbed like most people in the difficult task of rearing babies and making both ends meet. We left the aristocracy of art for the democracy of family life.

After our honeymoon spent in Assisi, we hoped—or rather I did—to spend our holidays travelling all over Europe. We never went further than Belgium. This was the end of my search for happiness, the closing chapter of romance, the sudden revelation of reality.

·　　·　　·　　·　　·

The reader may have wondered why I indulge in this account of matrimonial experiences in a chapter entitled

Liberalism and Christianity. The reason for this is very simple.

To a man brought up in an atmosphere of romantic humanism, true Christianity remains inaccessible unless he discards his romanticism and his humanism. It is impossible for him to experience faith, still less to enter the Church, unless he has been brought face to face with life, its joys and pains and countless worries. Christianity does not thrive in hothouses. The Gospel is almost aggressively unromantic, it does not deal with a dream, but with a terrible and wonderful truth, in which both joy and pain are intimately associated.

There is, however, a type of Christianity which may, to a certain extent, be reconciled with Romanticism and Humanism. This so-called liberal Christianity is by no means the Christianity of the Gospel, the religion of the Middle Ages or the true religion of to-day. Those whose belief is shaken by modern criticism are apt to seek refuge in this sentimental garden; those who are struggling towards divine faith, after indulging in secular creeds, are also tempted to linger there, and to rest in the shade of romantic rockeries. True Christianity, the Christianity of the Cross, is uncompromising. It does not belong to art, poetry or idealism. It is as real as the wood of which the Cross was made, as the nails which were hammered into the Cross, or the thorns which crowned Christ, Jesus Himself, true Man and true God.

Before joining the Church, a man should dare to live a true life. By this I do not mean that he must be "true to himself," but that he should no longer avoid the brutal facts which confront him in the family and the society to which he belongs.

This is why I was only baptized when I was over thirty years old, and why I only joined the Church of England seven years after I began to call myself a Christian in Belgium.

II

It is often said that the Reformation was a movement of emancipation, opposed to the teaching of the mediaeval Schoolmen, and that it should be considered as the religious expression of sixteenth century Humanism.

This generalisation is misleading. The revolt of Luther and Calvin against some of the teachings and many of the practices of the Church of Rome was in the one way encouraged by the critical attitude of Erasmus, but in another it was a reaction against the neo-pagan tendencies of the Renaissance, its exaltation of the joy of life and worship of beauty and riches. The refined and learned followers of Erasmus who tried to reform the Church from within were crushed between the fanaticism of the monks and the fanaticism of the Iconoclasts. From one point of view, the Reformation was a reaction against the slackness of a decadent Church which, through humanistic influences, tended to neglect the authority of the Scriptures and to avoid the stern consequences of human sin. From another point of view, the schism brought about by the conflict which tore Christianity asunder, weakened the authority of the Church and favoured rationalism. The worshippers of the Renaissance, in the South, by "restoring" Gothic buildings in the new style, and covering with whitewash mediaeval frescoes, co-operated with the Iconoclasts and the Puritans, in the North, in destroying invaluable monuments of mediaeval art. Christianity was soon divided between the Catholic humanists of the Counter Reformation who clung to papal authority, but sought inspiration in Seneca and Epictetus, and a number of Protestant sects who jealously preserved their independence and emphasized—and sometimes overemphasized—one aspect of the Scriptures at the expense of another. By the beginning of the nineteenth century, the Protestant churches in Northern Europe began to "humanize" their doctrine and to favour a new form of Christianity which could be reconciled with liberal enlightenment. About the same time, the Church of Rome, in spite of its strong traditions, by appealing to human sentiment over reason, drifted in the same direction. Just as the cleavage between Church and State may be more easily traced in Catholic countries, the development of this new form of Christianity, generally called "liberal," is more evident in Protestant countries where believers and unbelievers remained in close contact, and where the temptation to make greater concessions to the "spirit of the times" was consequently stronger.

.   .   .   .

Mediaeval Christianity was, on the whole, faithful to the tradition of the Church. Its interpreters, whether writers or artists, aimed at "teaching the Faith." Their work was a work of evangelisation which endeavoured to translate faithfully the essential features of Christian doctrine, from the Creation and the Fall to the Resurrection and the miraculous action of the Holy Ghost through the Church. God appeared as Creator and as Redeemer, and Christ Himself, as Man and as Judge. Indeed the same features were given to the Deity in these two aspects and it is significant that no distinction was made in art between the features of the Father and those of the Son until the beginning of the Renaissance.

The same spirit pervades all mediaeval civilisation. Whether we consider religious writings, paintings, sculpture or architecture, we are struck by this quality of directness, this unity of purpose. Modern scholarship has entirely confirmed Ruskin's statement that a cathedral is a "carved Bible." Mediaeval artists and writers were working under the supervision of the Church. They were not concerned with the pleasant or unpleasant nature of their works, and did not consider themselves qualified to emphasize one aspect of the Christian faith at the expense of another, or to discriminate between the traditional subjects they were commissioned to deal with. As a fourteenth century charter of the painters of Siena puts it, their task was to "teach religion to the people."

It may be objected that this teaching was no longer in accordance with the tradition of the early Church, or with that of the Bible, that some of the stories recorded were apocryphal, and that some of the lives of the saints were legendary; but that did not affect the spirit in which they were told. Due importance was given to the prophetic character of the Old Testament and to the episodes which express it. A balance was preserved between the human and the divine character of Christ, who appears as Man and Redeemer in the various episodes of His life on earth, and as God and Judge in the representation of the Last Judgment inspired by the Apocalypse. The dramatic conflict between Good and Evil was shown in the story of the Passion and in the pictures of Heaven and Hell. However crude some of these pictures may appear to-day, they remain faithful to the spirit of the Gospel and preserve the necessary contrast between the joy and pain of Christianity, which we seek vainly in later works. The carvings and stained-glass windows of the French cathedrals and the fourteenth century frescoes of Italy provide the most adequate and orthodox illustrations of the Gospels which our civilisation has produced.

． ． ． ． ．

The effect of the change brought about by Humanism in religious art is more clearly marked in Italy than in the North. It takes place during the first part of the fifteenth century when belated mediaevalists, such as Fra Angelico, still faithful to the old tradition, paint side by side with the forerunners of the new school, which finds its full expression in the semi-pagan art of Botticelli.

This change may be summed up briefly if we substitute the expression "pleasing" for "teaching." Leaving all technical considerations aside, it may be said that, while the mediaeval artists aimed at teaching the truth, the Renaissance artist's main preoccupation was to please his public. While the first endeavoured to picture religious events as they happened, or as he sincerely believed that they happened, and to instruct thereby the congregation, the second endeavoured to show his knowledge of forms and colours and to stir admiration. The artist superseded the teacher. Instead of insisting on the essential features of his religious subject, he multiplied picturesque incidents and introduced in the foreground the portraits of his patrons. As a rule, the Church encouraged rather than discouraged the new school, and within fifty years the mediaeval tradition was forgotten. The only important reaction was that of Savonarola whose preaching is supposed to have prompted Botticelli to burn in public some of his works.

The result was not only the introduction of pagan pictures and pagan literature into the palaces of the aristocracy and of the high clergy, but the introduction into the churches of religious pictures painted in a humanistic spirit. The Virgin Mary was portrayed simply as the smiling young mother bending over her baby. John the Baptist was no longer the austere prophet crying in the wilderness, but the small playfellow of the Child Jesus. The Nativity became more prominent than the Passion. The beautiful penitent Magdalene was given a leading part. The Last Supper lost its sacramental significance. Christ

Himself became a human hero, the innocent victim of a great betrayal. In short, the Gospel story received at best a purely epic and at worst a purely sentimental interpretation. This process of humanisation can be traced right through the sixteenth century in Italy and the seventeenth century in Flanders. It loses much of its interest after the display of Rubens' great decorative canvasses.[1]

The same change may be followed step by step in Western Europe, with regard to religious sculpture and architecture, from the Gothic to the early Renaissance style, and from the latter to the Baroque. It is not so evident in literature, because writers and preachers were more independent than artists of the fashion of the period in which they lived, and because they were divided, even within the Roman Church, between those, like the Jesuits, who favoured the change, and those, like the Jansenists, who opposed it. This change is nevertheless sufficiently apparent during the seventeenth and eighteenth centuries to confirm our conclusion that, in spite of temporary reactions, Christian humanism was gaining ground everywhere and threatened the Churches from within, as secular humanism threatened them from without.

This danger which was revealed clearly more than a century ago in Lutheran circles by Kierkegaard, and which has been denounced lately by many leading theologians, took the most varied forms, from superstitious pietism to religious "modernism." It has nevertheless some features which can easily be recognized. The keynote has already been struck: an anxiety to please instead of an

---

[1] I am not concerned here with the individual genius of the artists, but merely with the fact that this genius is not disciplined by tradition; the *religious* quality of their work is no longer equal to their artistic value. Rubens was a very devout man but he lived in a period when it had become impossible to paint a deeply religious picture. Baroque beauty cannot be true to the spirit of the Gospel.

eagerness to teach, propaganda instead of evangelisation. A moment came when Christians sacrificed so much to the spirit of the time—a spirit essentially hostile to Christianity—that the treasure of Church traditions accumulated for fifteen centuries seemed practically exhausted. It was a race against time, and it was doubtful whether Christianity did not face a greater danger at the hands of its supporters than at the hands of its adversaries. Religious defeatism was halted partly by the reaction provoked by the last war, which caused among Christians a return to first principles, and partly by the development of modern scientific philosophy, which took the bitterness from the conflict between science and religion. But the enemy is still within the gates and, at the risk of repeating what has been said recently by a number of specialists, it might be useful to outline his main features.

. . . . .

The "anxiety to place" was either negative or positive. In its negative form, it eliminated or minimized the aspects of the Christian doctrine which offended the spirit of scientific rationalism prevalent in the nineteenth century. In its positive form, it exaggerated or distorted those aspects which could lend themselves to pleasant expression, stir up religious emotionalism, and provide the worshipper with a feeling of moral uplift and physical security. The result was a kind of vague religiosity deprived of intellectual backbone and prone to indulge in self-pity and self-complacency, a religiosity which aroused and to some extent deserved the attacks of the materialists who denounced it as "dope."

The negative aspect came to the fore when it was found necessary to parry the blows of those who attacked religion in general, and Christianity in particular. The first attack was delivered under the banner of Reason, the goddess of the French Jacobins. It was bound to fail because the worship of a human faculty combined with a vague belief in providence could not exert any popular appeal. The second attack was delivered under the banner of Science and culminated in the Darwinian controversy.

As this controversy developed, it challenged the historical character of the New Testament and the whole question of belief in the supernatural. What lay at the back of the criticism which pervaded intellectual circles during the last century, was the conviction, amounting to a faith, that any manifestation of the supernatural is a conclusive proof of the unhistorical character of the event recorded. The modern tendency to give way to popular opinion in order to safeguard a last stronghold of moral principles did far more harm to Christianity than the bitterest attacks to which it was subjected. These were bound to wear off—as they did in fact wear off as soon as leading scientists frankly recognized the limitation of scientific enquiry. Spiritual defeatism, on the contrary, increased with every strategical retreat. As a number of miracles were either questioned or explained away without sufficient justification, the supernatural authority which was the very foundation of the Christian faith was severely shaken. After doubting the miraculous cures recorded in the Gospel, people doubted the Incarnation, the Resurrection and the redeeming value of the Crucifixion. The creation and the fall of man were discarded or glossed over. What remained for a large number of people who called themselves Christians was the tragic story of a man and the moral teaching he had given to his disciples. He was acknowledged to have been "the best man who ever lived," and his "message" was considered as the most "uplifting" ever taught. But both truth and authority had been eliminated. The work of humanisation was complete. Christ was no longer God made man, but a certain man made God by his pious admirers. His commandments were no longer absolute; they were relative to the period and to the circumstances in which he lived, and their authority could be questioned in any other period or circumstances. His words and actions could be criticized as those of any other prophet or philosopher. The worst consequence of this abject retreat was that the very claim to infallibility and divine authority which Christ had made in His own name and in the name of His Father could no longer be upheld.[2]

Again and again, the modernists who had initiated this movement within the Churches were condemned by the hierarchy, or endeavoured themselves to call a halt. But they had no longer any ground on which to make a stand. Having given up the key position of supernatural authority, they were unable to resist the impetus of the movement which assailed them. Some of them sought refuge in personal religious experience, but such experience has no positive value. Mysticism may lead to new discoveries, when based on sound doctrine, it is a weak line of retreat when the stronghold of dogma has already capitulated.

This brief outline of the negative policy pursued by liberal Christianity in the hope of safeguarding "Christian principles" may appear exaggerated to-day, because we are already benefiting from the reaction which followed. It will not appear exaggerated to those who remember the dark days through which Christianity passed during the first decade of this century. Now that science has recognized its limitations and that religious thinkers realize that no scientific discovery can affect their faith in Christ,

[2] The greatest exponent of Liberal Christianity is perhaps Ernest Renan. Brought up in a seminary, he left the Church and wrote a series of books which exercised a strong influence on his contemporaries. There are in *La Vie de Jésus* (1863) a number of statements which were accepted by many Protestants at the time.

as He manifests Himself in the world and in the Church, the old conflict may be considered at an end. The position of both believer and unbeliever has been clarified, as far as reason is concerned. Where faith is concerned, however, no compromise is possible. The supernatural element is as essential to religion as free investigation is essential to science. It is the foundation of all dogma, the source of all moral authority. Christ is God *and* Man, or He is nothing. The spiritual value of the Gospel depends on the Incarnation and the Resurrection, and both Incarnation and Resurrection are dependent on the doctrine of the Redemption, which itself implies the fall of man and original sin. The whole edifice rests on these four columns. To sacrifice any of them in order to allay a passing prejudice is to shake the whole framework of a Creed established for two thousand years.

Experience has shown that time alone can heal such divisions, and time is on the side of the eternal truths. But experience has also shown that it is extremely dangerous to discard such truths in a vain attempt to reconcile the irreconcilable.

.   .   .   .

Liberal Christianity did not only endeavour to minimize every fact or idea which revealed the supernatural nature of the Faith, its dogmatic and authoritative character, it also emphasized every fact or idea which increased its sentimental appeal. Its most popular authors of sermons and hymns insist, at one and the same time, on allowing more freedom of interpretation and on developing a feeling of moral and physical security. This positive action did almost as much harm as the negative action which we have just described.

The problem of teaching religion to the young has

always been a difficult one and those who have tried to cope with it know the risks which must be taken in initiating children to the realisation of sin, for instance, and to the story of the Crucifixion. A healthy Christian spirit cannot be fostered in children by inspiring them with an exaggerated sense of guilt, a morbid terror of the Devil or a hysterical pity for the physical torments of martyrs.

At the end of the last century, however, the pendulum swung to the other extreme. It was said that the children's "purity" should not be tarnished by the knowledge of evil, and that the only picture of Christianity which should be presented to them should be an entirely happy one. It was added that Christ Himself had sanctified the little ones' innocence when he urged His disciples to let them come unto Him, "for of such is the Kingdom of Heaven." There is evidence in the Gospels that Christ showed a child's readiness to believe as an example to the adult, but He never mentioned the "childlike sinlessness" so much in favour during the romantic period. The opinion prevailed nevertheless, that any allusion to temptation and sin in a nursery or a Sunday School was harming the child's soul by imparting to him the knowledge of things the existence of which he did not even suspect. It was therefore agreed that the "purity" of the young should be respected, and that their "natural love of goodness" should rest undisturbed. As this love of goodness was merely theoretical, the teacher and parents were compelled to substitute for a moral discipline, resting on reasonable principles, a personal appeal or a threat of punishment which could not exert any lasting influence. The main thing was to build up in the child's mind a rosy picture of Christianity which he could always remember in later days.

He was first urged to turn to Jesus, in his cradle:

> Gentle Jesus, meek and mild,
> Look upon a little child;
> Pity my simplicity,
> Suffer me to come to Thee.

Then, to lift his eyes to heaven:

> There's a friend for little children,
> Above the bright blue sky . . .

And to believe that if he loved God, his salvation was assured and his reward "prepared":

> And if I now earnestly seek Him below,
> I shall see Him and hear Him above:
> In that beautiful place He has gone to prepare
> For all that are washed and forgiven.

The same scrupulous delicacy of feeling was shown in the interpretation of the Crucifixion, in the well-known hymn beginning with the words: "There is a green hill far away":

> We may not know, we cannot tell
> What pains He had to bear,
> But we believe it was for us
> He hung and suffer'd there.

It is useless to dwell here on the danger of shirking in this way the most important questions with which the Christian has to deal. We should do well to compare this hymn to the spirit in which St. Francis received the Holy Stigmata on Mount Verna. When the boy remembers these pictures of his childhood and compares them with his experience as an adolescent, he must necessarily feel that they have little connection with real life, and that they "belong to the nursery."

Some hope would remain of correcting this error, at a later stage, if these hymns, which are unfortunately the most popular, were strictly reserved for the young. The tragedy is that the style of a large number of "general hymns" seems directly inspired by them. We find again and again the same assurance, the same apparent complacency, the same desire to extract from Christianity the maximum comfort and security.

Here is a Christian praying for the forgiveness of his sins:

> Pour down upon us from above
> The riches of Thy pardoning love.
> Remember, O Lord, though frail we be,
> That yet thine handiwork are we:
> Nor let the honour of Thy Name
> Be by another put to shame.

Or lost in contemplation, at the time of the Passion:

> Truly blessed is the station,
> Low before His Cross to lie,
> Whilst I see Divine compassion
> Beaming in His languid eye.

Or hoping for the reward of his piety:

> Eternal glory, rest on high,
> A blessèd immortality,
> True peace and gladness, and a throne,
> Are all His gifts and all our own.

Sentimentalism and self-satisfaction are the sure symptoms of a decadent Christianity. To exploit the physical suffering of Christ, we must have become ignorant of His spiritual suffering. To exploit the promise of reward, we must have lost all sense of humility. In its worst aspects Liberal Christianity almost agrees with Humanism. The first lowers the stature of God, the second raises the stature of Man.

. . . . . .

It is a painful task to dwell on the weakness of an attitude which is still sincerely shared by a large number of devout and admirable Christians. We are sometimes properly warned that it is dangerous to expose even a weak religion. I can unfortunately only accept this warning if I recognize this weakness. Complacency, in such matters, does not only imply the betrayal of Christian duty, it implies the surrender of the whole Christian position. The direct result of the negative and positive efforts made by well-meaning Christians, in order to preserve the acceptance of Christian morals and to "fill the churches," has been to empty them of a large and increasing number of people who have been brought into contact with the brutal realities of modern life and who are determined to face them. These people, especially among the younger generation, have been led to believe that a religion which expresses itself in such a vague and "sloppy" language is only suitable for the very young or the very old, and that it cannot inspire the courage which fills their own souls. They are inclined to scorn a faith which "plays for safety" and which favours escapism. They refuse to accept the existence of a supernatural world which appears to them to have no connection with the hard world which confronts them. This attitude is as arrogant as the type of religion which it condemns is weak, but it must be treated with the same understanding because life to-day is neither pleasing nor secure and compels the young to make cruel sacrifices, which are not made less cruel by pious promises. They have grown up in an atmosphere of disillusionment and do not wish to indulge in further illusions. They have reached a point where the pleasant character given to Christianity fills them with suspicion and where every attempt made to render religion more attractive confirms their conviction that it has no bearing upon the personal and social problems with which they have to deal.

In spite of the sympathy we feel for those who cling to cherished memories, we should recognize that the attitude of unbelievers to-day is to a certain extent explained by some manifestations of modern belief. If Christianity is only a refuge for those whose worldly hopes and ambitions have been disappointed, if its principal quality is to be not only comforting but "comfortable," morally and physically, if its aim is to add a spiritual home to our temporal home, in which we shall recover and preserve for ever those things which are and have been dearest to us—then this religion is indeed remote from these catastrophic days, in which love and tragedy walk side by side under the shadow of famine and death, in which the old world is crumbling down before a new one can even be "planned," and ancient conventions and safeguards are shattered by a succession of devastating storms. This is no time for safety-first religion. It is a time for self-denial and moral humility, a time very similar to the first centuries of Christian life.

By catering for the selfish and timorous attitude of the modern man, and especially of the nineteenth century bourgeois, liberal Christians made an error common to most propagandists. They underestimated the moral value of their public. However sinful he may be, the common man retains a desire to rise to the occasion. In one way he is attached to security, in another he is attracted by danger. In one way he clings to his moral and material possessions, in another he is inclined to take risks. From the early years of persecution to modern times, Christianity has always stood for dangerous living. It has always combined a healthy love of life with a healthier desire to sacrifice it, for the love of God. This paradox has inspired the spreading of the Gospel throughout history; it dominates the age of chivalry; it stands as an unforgettable ideal behind the bold and generous action of all those missionaries who abandoned a sheltered life to feed the poor, nurse the sick, deliver the slave and succour the afflicted. True Christians have always considered themselves as pilgrims in this world. At any moment the call may come which compels them to leave their home and to shoulder their burden or their cross. The love of one's neighbour is not inspired by pity. It is inspired by the unquenchable thirst for adventure, by the passionate desire to give up everything, wealth, family, friendship, and to devote oneself body and soul, to the service of God. For the Love of God is a jealous and exclusive love which does not admit rival claims. If there is one duty which is stressed more than another in the Gospel, it is this exclusiveness: "These are my mother and brothers," "Let the dead bury their dead," "For he had great possessions." Only those who are ready to leave everything when His voice is heard are given grace to follow the Master.

Those who, in their anxiety to make religion palatable to the weak, contend that the old rule does not apply to modern circumstances are flying in the face of Christian tradition. They are trying to serve two masters. No social or political change, no scientific discovery, can alter the fact that, if our life ceases to be dangerous, it ceases also to be Christian. There is no life which requires greater courage, greater determination, more patience and constancy, because its strength is founded upon the rock of an absolute faith. Neither pride, nor ambition can help the Christian; he must find his way in all humility, and follow it with complete disregard for the material results achieved. There is no promise of reward or success in this world, and the disproportion between the Love of God and man's ability to answer it, is so great that salvation must always appear a somewhat remote possibility. The Christian can believe in the Truth, he can never be sure of following it as it should be followed.

This is the hard, virile faith of St. Peter and St. Paul which has been made so soft and easy by those who placed quantity above quality, and wished to smooth the way under the delicate feet of the present generation. The present generation's answer has been to leave the way. Had it been shown for what it really was and always has been, a steep rocky path to be followed on bleeding feet in the stark nakedness of humility and contrition, this desertion might have been prevented.

. . . .

Christianity is above all heroic and consistent. By throwing a discreet veil on human sinfulness and on the supernatural powers of God, as Creator and Judge, liberal Christianity undermined the very foundations of the Church. By making heroism the monopoly of saints and mystics, it removed from the people the main motive power of their devotion. These two features of the faith, in its theoretical and practical interpretation, are closely linked together, and it is easy to understand that those who minimize the one should also minimize the other.

It needs some courage for a man bred and born in the modern world to accept a miracle, and the doctrine which is the logical consequence of that miracle. But the acceptance of this miracle and of this doctrine is the very essence of religion. After trying for four centuries every kind of compromise by imposing an arbitrary moral code on an immoral world, or by eliminating from religion every feature which proved objectionable to the majority, we have reached a point when only two attitudes are possible: the rejection or the acceptance of supernatural power. The first leads to materialism estimated in temporal values, the second to Christianity estimated in spiritual values.

The loss of prestige of Christianity among the young may be measured to-day by the fact that to most of them it appears at the same time more "realistic" and more "plucky" to be a Communist than to be an active member of the Church. Quite apart from other considerations, concerning the historical existence of Jesus and the reliability of the Gospel, it seems incredible that a belief which takes into account death as well as life, pain as well as joy, should be considered as more remote from reality than a philosophy which limits its scope to temporal life and leaves unanswered the most fundamental problems of human destiny. And it seems still more incredible that a faith which implies the immediate and complete sacrifice of all worldly goods and affections should need less courage than a political conviction which aims precisely at increasing the material and moral comfort of the majority. If to-morrow a bishop dropped his crook in order to wield the pickaxe of a laborer, people might criticize him for relinquishing his post, but no one would be entitled to suggest that his action was inconsistent with his faith. If the Chief Commissar of a Communistic Republic or the Prime Minister of any modern State resigned on the ground that he wished to work in a factory, the reaction would be very different, for there is no article in any political creed which allows the most influential member of the community to abandon the privileges and responsibilities of power. The bishop might justify his attitude by that of practically every saint in the Christian calendar; the Commissar or the Prime Minister could not easily discover a precedent.

The supernatural character of the Christian faith is constantly emphasized by those who refuse to accept its stern realism, but it is precisely this supernatural character which causes such sternness. There is no absolute authority to be found in this world. Every scientific achievement is determined by the results of research, which may soon be modified by the results of further research. Every political principle is determined by social and economic experiments which may be altered by fresh experiments. In the natural world, we find ourselves in the realm of relative conditions subject to change, and allowing some concessions and compromises. In the supernatural world, we have to deal not only with hard spiritual facts, such as the Incarnation and the Resurrection, but with absolute and eternal doctrines involving definite Commandments, such as the love of God and of one's neighbour, which may be extremely difficult to follow, but which cannot possibly be distorted in the light of passing circumstances. Virtue may be the monopoly of the saints, although no saint worthy of the name would ever admit it; it is certainly not the monopoly of the average Christian. But there is this capital difference between the atheist and the Christian: the atheist can always modify his standard according to the changeable conditions of a changing world; the Christian is bound to obey orders which were given to man two thousand years ago and which will have the same authority in another two thousand years. The validity of these orders may be challenged, but the severity of the discipline which they impose on those who dare to accept them is unchallengeable.

VI.

THE IMPACT OF PAIN

I

I TRIED TO EXPLAIN IN THE LAST CHAPTER HOW THE experience of a deep and lasting joy in marriage delivered me from dreamland, and brought me for the first time into contact with the realities of life.

Many Christians can find in happiness a solid foundation for their faith, for a great and deep joy brings to those who have been trained in the worship of God a fullness of spiritual life which implies the possible impact of pain. Charity entails sharing the joy and pains of others, and there is so much sorrow in the world that it is not easy to imagine how those who practise charity can possibly avoid the experience of sorrow, even if they are fortunate enough to be spared this experience in their private lives. Joy, therefore, should be enough, whether derived from marriage or from other sources, such as the exercise of a vocation.

But my religion was neither disciplined, nor unselfish. After a few years of spiritual exaltation, following my baptism and confirmation, I became irregular in religious observances and I felt more and more inclined to consider the Church as a benevolent mother whose mission it was to help my individual efforts, instead of the Kingdom of God on earth whose laws, as a good citizen, it was my duty to obey. I was still the kind of Christian who tries to get from the Church more than he gives, who likes to see his children baptised and confirmed, who wishes to attend a

120

service, particularly when it is a "good service," and who does not realize that the quality of the ceremony which he is impertinent enough to criticize, does not depend only on the priest, or on the choir and organist, but also on the traditional prayers of the Church, including his own—not on what he receives, but on what by grace he should be able to give.

On the other hand, my life became more and more absorbed in my home, and I was inclined to limit the number of my acquaintances, in order that the family circle should not be broken. I fell into the trap opened under the feet of many "good" fathers who believe that they have fulfilled their responsibility, because they have sacrificed their personal pleasures or ambitions to their wife and children. I deluded myself in thinking that my love for them was unselfish, while I derived an unlimited selfish pleasure in finding myself the centre of their attention. This new worship or mutual worship was certainly real, and was not tainted with the humanitarian idealism which had marred my worship of nature, art and "mankind," but it was by no means innocent. It is not sinful to love one's wife and children, but it is sinful to love them to the exclusion of other people, and it is still more sinful to allow this love to divert one's attention from the love of God.

My faith was too superficial to thrive on happiness alone. Life, with me, although deeply real, remained one-sided. I loved my work, took delight in my leisure, and was relatively free from money troubles. I could even afford to give my children what is supposed to be a sound education, and what is certainly a very expensive one. God, I thought, blessed my efforts, and because He blessed them, I rashly assumed that they deserved to be blessed. I supposed that I had reached the end of my journey and that I could soon rest in security and contentment. Such delusion may be compared to that of an inexperienced climber who thinks he has reached almost the top of the pass after emerging from the woods which cover the slopes of the mountain, while he has still to face the longer and steeper part of his climb, among the desolation of rocks and snow.

. . . .

If anyone had suggested, twenty years ago, that I had not experienced suffering, I would have answered that I had paid my debt during the last war, when I had been separated from my mother and brother who remained in Brussels, and had witnessed the cruel ordeal which afflicted my own people. Had I not suffered then and expressed the suffering of my country in prose and verse, to the best of my ability? I would have been ready to admit that these efforts had little literary value, but I should have refused to recognize the fact that even the storm of the last war did not seriously disturb the serenity of my life.

It had been a tragic interval in the story of my happiness, four years of struggle, turmoil and excitement, a period of long waiting until the sky cleared again and pre-war activities might be resumed. The war seemed to me a straightforward fight between a permanent and all pervading good and a temporary evil which was monopolized by one nation and even by one class in one nation. Although the small knowledge of history I possessed should have prevented such wide generalisations, my reaction against imperial Germany's violation of Belgian territory had led me to over-simplify my views. No awkward doubt existed in my mind as to the responsibility for the conflict and its necessary conclusion. I considered the war not as the outcome of a Humanism and Nationalism four centuries old, but as an accident in the natural progress of mankind. My politics had not kept pace with my religion. Like many of my contemporaries, I suffered from a lack of co-ordination between my individual and political ideas. If I was closer to reality in my personal life, I was still, as a citizen, indulging in a vague idealism far remote from historical experience. While, as an individual, I had discarded Utopia several years before the outbreak of war, as a citizen, I continued to nurse the most foolish illusions several years after its conclusion. I scarcely realized that I lived in two worlds which were in flagrant contradiction with each other: my country and my home, the dangerous dream of a world from which a recent victory had eradicated economic competition and national ambition, and the pleasant reality of a family whose security depended on the realisation of this dream.

Three children were born to us between 1914 and 1919. We fully realized the risk we were taking in increasing our responsibilities in such unsettled circumstances, but we were taking this risk in the conviction that, whatever happened, our children would not have their lives upset by another war. We thought ourselves very brave in challenging fate in this way. Fate, or the natural forces which bring about retribution for every individual and collective error or sin, accepted our challenge, and the blow fell twenty years later.

. . . . . .

Nothing shows better the impotence of people whose decisions are inspired by humanistic principles than the study of the long crisis which separates the two world wars. The peacemakers of 1918-1919 had apparently the world at their feet, but even if they had been the most saintly men the nations which they represented were in no mood to accept decisions inspired by Christian charity and justice.

The majority, even among Christians, were still hypnotised by the blind faith in the fundamental goodness of man. They could not deny the recent catastrophe, but they denied that they had a share of responsibility for its outbreak. This crime had been committed by one nation waylaid by a certain number of people belonging to a certain government. It would be enough to remove the representatives of this government, paralyse the evil forces which it had set to work, and re-educate the people, in order to remove all danger from that quarter. Since all the other nations, and especially the Allied nations, were by definition "good nations," they would not be likely to follow the bad example given by their common enemy. Besides, in order to make assurance doubly sure, they would sign a Covenant in which they would undertake to help each other against any would-be aggressor. International Law would be restored for an indefinite period of time.[1]

This was the humanistic attitude in 1918, as it still is, to a great extent, the humanistic attitude to-day. According to it, the only remedy which can be found against a future war in this world consists in fixing the responsibility for the conflict on one of the belligerents, in punishing its leaders and in signing solemn treaties which are supposed to prevent the recurrence of the catastrophe. Such a remedy, however, cannot possibly cure the disease, because those who use it refuse to recognize its fundamental cause: human sin.

In contrast to the humanist majority, a few "realists" had the courage to maintain that, although "human nature" does not always "remain the same," international competition interrupted by the war, would soon resume

[1] See Professor Carr's "The Twenty Years' Crisis," *passim*.

its course, even between ex-Allies. Such competitions would either lead to a conflict between old friends, or to a new conflict against the old enemies, if the latter were able to exploit these divisions. The voice of these realists was not heard, partly because it expressed an unpleasant truth and partly because it had no alternative proposal to offer. It was strong in destructive criticism, but weak in constructive statesmanship. No sound policy, based on spiritual and material reality, was opposed to the post-war illusion about the magic value of the League or other international systems.

I had had serious doubts about the efficiency of these systems before 1925, but the failure of Locarno, under the impact of the economic crisis of 1929, left no doubt in my mind as to the forthcoming crisis. From that moment, I understood that I could no longer reconcile my political views with my personal convictions, that no connection existed between Utopia and realism either in political or in personal affairs.

As the clouds darkened the horizon during the last years which preceded the second war, and as I felt more and more certain that only a miracle could save Europe and my home from the new catastrophe which threatened them, I applied myself to readjusting my conceptions of the world to the events I was witnessing. I saw at last that, in spite of the experience I had acquired, I had allowed my optimism to carry me beyond the limits of wisdom, and that my views had been unduly influenced by my reluctance to acknowledge the hard fact of sin and its consequences.

As a young man, I had refused to accept reality, because it implied pain for myself and for others. As a father, I had only accepted that part of reality which implied the hope of avoiding pain, if not for myself, at least for those who were closest to me. As an old man, I was at last impelled to recognize that joy and pain are the very core of an individed truth, and should both be accepted with courage and resignation. And it began to dawn upon me that the only chance of increasing the one and reducing the other was to admit the existence of both frankly and unquestioningly. The teaching of Christianity was no longer for me a guide to happiness, or a blessing conferred upon happiness as a reward for virtue; it was a complete surrender to the will of God. Only through that surrender and that acceptance could man discover, not the peace of this world, but some human approximation to the peace "which passeth all understanding."

This fundamental necessity of "saying yes to God" had been shown to me by another English prophet who probed much deeper into the problems of his own generation than Ruskin ever did. The grief I felt at the loss of my friend G. K. Chesterton led me to re-read his works and to praise his teaching in a small book which was an inadequate tribute to his true greatness.[2] Many people only appreciated his healthy laughter, but the time will come when more people will understand the wisdom hidden behind that laughter.

. . . . . .

We are apt to think that there is something providential in the events of our life. It is no doubt flattering to believe that a loving Providence takes us by the hand and points out to us the various stages of our journey on earth. But if we only kept our eyes and ears open, we would soon understand that, in most cases, life itself is our providence. It is enough to observe the world with an unclouded mind, and to experience joy and suffering without feeling that we deserve or do not deserve them, to reach the conviction that our own development is bound up with the world's

[2] The Laughing Prophet, 1937.

development. "Why of yourselves judge ye not what is right?"

The best advice which could be given to any young man or woman would be to urge him not to allow his present beliefs, whatever they may be, to harden into prejudice, to keep an open mind, to watch eagerly what happens to him and around him, and never to close the book of life before reading the last page. There is no more fatal error than to imagine that our education is completed in school and university. We should always be at school, we should always prepare for some examination, until the final examination. A secular life tends to narrow our outlook because it induces us to close the book after reading the first chapter. A Christian life compels us to leave the book open to the end. Should we do otherwise, we would cease to be Christian.[3]

It would be dishonest to say that, as an old man, I have no pride left. I am far too human to be able to make such a statement. But my greatest pride is perhaps that I never closed the book of life or that, if I did, I hastened to reopen it. I am not entirely responsible for this, and no doubt the spirit of discovery helped me to keep both book and mind open, and so to allow "providence" to teach me my lesson, chapter by chapter, and to correct my errors blunder by blunder.

I wish to emphasize this point, because some readers may think that in my attacks against Humanism and other errors, I have indulged in the modern fashion of "debunking" great things and great men. Nothing has been further from my mind. What I have tried to do is to show that however great the thing, there is a greater thing, and however great the man, or the truth expounded by the man, there is a greater truth. I have worshipped in many temples and I may regret having spent so much time in some of

[3] Concerning religious dogma, *see* p. 64.

them, but I do not regret possessing the spirit of admiration and worship. This spirit is my only safeguard against error, and it is only with it and through it that I may presume to kneel at last in God's own temple, the One Holy Catholic and Apostolic Church, the Church of the Creed.

. . . .

I have reached what I firmly believe to be the last chapter in the story of my life, which will also be the last chapter of this book. There remains, however, a very important experience to relate which did more than anything else to prepare me for the death of my brother, the humiliation of my King and country, and the loss of my second son, killed in the R.A.F.[4] Within a few months, I was struck in my closest personal affections, in deep rooted patriotic loyalties and in the work to which I had devoted most of my activity: the furthering of friendly relations between England and Belgium. I am still wondering how I avoided despair and how my suffering was converted into a strengthened hope and an ineradicable faith. This did not certainly happen through my own power, but if God helped me, as I am sure He did, how was it that, after my long and varied life, I preserved enough resilience to accept such blows and, through my acceptance, obtain such help?

It was no doubt, once more, through the example of my wife who through this crisis, as through all the crises of our life together, stood beside me unflinchingly. During these months, more than at any other time, I felt the benefit of her mistaken confidence in the strength of my own character. I was determined that she should not be disappointed, and by trying to appear steadfast, I succeeded at least in avoiding the pitfalls of self-pity and

[4] *Upon this Rock.*

emotionalism. But I received other help from another quarter.

The relationship of parents and children is often compared to that of birds and their young. When the young are able to fly and to feed themselves, they leave the old nest and start life on their own. This, it is argued, is what should happen in the human family. If children and parents parted in time it would prevent friction and heartburnings. The only flaw in this argument is that men differ from beasts, even from the most homely beasts. Adolescent boys are not in a position to earn their own living and rear a family. Among civilised people and especially in the professional classes, there is, for good or evil, a long stage during which the children remain at home, at least during the holidays, while they are "equipping themselves for life." The so-called "natural severance of family ties" is therefore unduly delayed and, whether they like it or not, parents and children are thrown back on each other until the young find some regular employment or marry.

This is usually a period of tension because, on the one hand, the father and mother are seldom able to treat their growing children as independent beings, and because, on the other, the children chafe against an authority which hampers their movement—even if it is a purely moral authority. The situation is complicated by the possessiveness of parental affection and by the memory of father- and mother-worship. The most united families are often the most seriously affected.

I should not go so far as to say that our home was spared these growing pains of emancipation, but mutual affection was such that our children gave us time to readjust ourselves to the new situation, and to abdicate our power without suffering too much from the pangs of abdication. In some instances, we agreed to differ, in others the parents benefited from the children's influence and learnt from them as much as they had been able to teach them in the heyday of their moral and intellectual prestige. For, if in the animal world connections are necessarily interrupted, so that the parents may rear another family, in the human world they are and should be prolonged in order that the parents' education might be completed.

And so it happened that some of my children, who had been in close touch at university with the Student Christian Movement, were able to help me by introducing me to a number of authors and to a few friends who showed me that, in spite of my assumed realism, I had by no means been purged from humanistic illusions.

As the menace of impending war grew, every year, every month, I was able to alter the centre of gravity of my mind from joy, under God, to joy and pain, under God, and from virtue marred by sin, to sin redeemed by virtue. I learned something about the Kingdom of God and its actual significance, how our present life is not completely cut off from our future life, and how both are part of life everlasting. As my anxiety became more and more acute, I was gradually given the armour which would protect me from the blows which I was going to receive, and the weapons with which I would fight the despair and bitterness which might follow. As the bad news from this world showed that the catastrophe could no longer be avoided, the good news of the Gospel in which I read more than I had ever read before, showed the continuity of temporal and eternal life, the infinite power of redemption, the external justice and mercy of God, the utter humility with which His judgment should be accepted by man.

Theology is not an intellectual exercise to be opposed to mystical experience, it is the integration through human reason of a revealed truth. It may be superfluous for the saint or for those whose faith is so strong that it need not be tempered by reason, but it is indispensable for the common man, and for those whose questioning mind must organize the framework of a creed before acknowledging it. The neglect of theology by the ordinary reader has been one of the main causes of the Church's loss of power, as the recent interest shown in it is one of the hopeful signs of a Christian renaissance.

We have lost our way in a world of dreams and nightmares and must take our bearings again. We must rediscover the meaning and purpose of life in the service of God the true value of civilisation to His greater glory, the pain that chokes every cry of joy and the joy that fulfils the anguish of pain, the redeeming seeds of virtue embedded in every human sin, and the dangerous tares of sin rooted in every human virtue. We must be born again to a new God-centred world in which man may be freed from the oppression of his own ambition, of his own power, of his own importance. For man is only important because God created him in His own image and called him to His service. As man wanders away from this image, this love and this service, he may fill the earth with technical wonders, elaborate the most learned systems, even create the most impressive works of art, all his efforts will end in disaster, and dust will return to dust.

II

It has been said that the weakest feature of humanist philosophy is that the most important questions which dominate human life are beyond its scope, and that man cannot resign himself to leave unanswered such problems as the nature of his own being, his survival after death and the purpose of creation. But this is to assume that people are, on the one hand, gifted with an enquiring mind and, on the other, moved by the desire to base their individual and social life on sound beliefs.

A minority may be led back to Christianity through the failure of Humanism, but most people have scarcely been touched by such intellectual disillusionment. Most unbelievers remain unwilling to face questions which they are unprepared to answer, and ready to forget the latest shipwreck and embark on fresh adventures.

It is not true to say that man cannot live without a belief in God and a hope in eternal life. Millions have done so for generations. They have pushed aside problems which they called insoluble and hopes which they called fantastic, and they have done it for so long that they have ceased to think of death or life after death, and are content to live from year to year as if their short career would never end.

What is true is that man cannot live without any faith, and that, from the time he lost his belief in God, he has applied himself to build up a series of secular beliefs in Reason, Freedom, Individualism, Socialism, Nationalism, Internationalism, or Racialism, which are all different forms of Humanism. When we speak of the "religious instinct" we wrongly assume that this very real need must necessarily lead to a supernatural religion based on eternal truth. It may lead and has led now for four centuries to secular religions based on passing dogmas and on "orders" which are accepted and obeyed with as much zeal and devotion as if they were divine. It is not unfortunately in the nature of man to think straight, but it is in the nature of man, and especially of crowds, to adopt a creed and to sacrifice themselves to it. The quality of such creeds does not affect the fundamental truth of this statement. The most appalling heresies have had their martyrs.

·   ·   ·   ·   ·

Humanists have endeavoured again and again to give an ultimate aim to existence and to tear man away from mere hedonism. They strove to show that no social life could be founded on the gospel: "Eat, drink and be merry, for to-morrow we die." The Cartesians fought against it in the name of reason, the Romantics in the name of sensitivity; most people did not follow their lead because they refused to be guided by abstract ideology or by vague sentiment. The Socialists fought against hedonism in the name of solidarity and the crowd followed their lead because they hoped to find in human brotherhood alone the solution of their troubles. But solidarity soon became class solidarity, and the brothers, orphans who had no father to settle their differences. Individual interest, class interest, national interest scored every time, and the small band of liberal idealists who had let the flood loose were left stranded on their desert island, contemplating the results of the catastrophe they had unconsciously caused.

The masses are not wise, but they possess a certain common sense which can be ruthlessly logical. If "to-morrow we die," why should we not "eat, drink and be merry"? If death means nothing but corruption and total destruction, why should life mean anything more than the satisfaction of our own desires, whether these desires concern the individual, the class, the nation or the race? Why should we sacrifice anything to others if everything which gives us satisfaction is "good," and everything which deprives us of it is "bad"? What effort should we make to conform to any moral standard if morals are identified with "self-expression," and their "principles" subjected to constant change? Like Truth, Goodness should be eternal, and what significance does it retain if it alters according to the ups and downs of political and international conflict?

Idealism has only occasionally been practised by a small intellectual aristocracy; the majority may be moved by it for a time but, unless they embrace a real and eternal faith, they are bound to fall back again and again on the realistic and temporary claim of their generation. Liberalism was the logical expression of such a claim when political life was restricted to the moneyed classes. Totalitarianism, in its various forms, became the logical expression of the same claim when political life was extended to the whole people in a world without religion.

The present war is not merely a fight between democracy and autocracy, it is also a fight for the defence of certain ideas which were left in the background until they were directly challenged. It was caused by the instinctive reaction people felt when they were faced with the inevitable results of what they had themselves for so long called "progress" and "efficiency." For present-day democracy is only the result of a compromise between liberal capitalism and controlled socialism, which are both apt to degenerate into totalitarianism. Behind these hovers still, like a shadow in the distance, the symbol of a faith which for most men had already lost its original meaning. It was towards this shadow that people turned in 1938-1939, when they decided to resist the pressure of unavoidable circumstances. They suddenly declared that they were defending beliefs and principles which they had for long discarded. They realized that they were not so much fighting in order to preserve what they had won, as to retain a chance of recovering what they had lost. They felt compelled to oppose some ideal to that of the enemy and were necessarily driven, by their very hostility to the anti-Christian creed of Nazism, towards a reassertion of a faith they had almost forgotten. If the Cross is ever raised again on the solid rock of Europe, its reappearance will be due not so much to those who hoped to preserve it as to those who wished to destroy it for ever. Evangelisation, in the twentieth century, will not come so much from the admiration stirred by apostles and saints, as from the revulsion caused by sadists and tyrants. The Love of God converted the world two thousand years ago; we are beginning to wonder whether the hate of evil, in our enemies and in ourselves, may not lead us to a new conversion.

. . . .

This war has been an eye-opener in more senses than one. It has destroyed the illusion fostered by the worship of man: human goodness, human freedom, human progress, leading to an earthly paradise. It has revealed evil in all its horror, the cunning of the persecutor, the cruelty of the tormenter, the constant spying and bribing which tempt men and women to treason; it has also revealed the meaning of pain.

Most of us have watched rabbits playing in a field. If we have accompanied a shooting party, we must have seen the sudden start of the beast when wounded, and the trembling which followed before it was able to crawl under the bracken. Men do not differ from rabbits when they are hit. They stop playing, wondering what has happened to them; then, as the pain grows, they start trembling in awe and fear at the sudden realisation of their danger. We stopped playing in 1914, but we never lost the hope of resuming our game when "the nightmare was over." In 1939, we began to understand that the game itself was over, that we should be compelled not only during the war, but also after the war, to give up playing, to take life seriously and to face its stern realities.

The most real thing about life is death, just as the most real thing about joy is pain. Confronted with death and pain, man must choose between God and the world, the spirit and the flesh, Christianity and atheism. It is the dilemma of his destiny and it has taken four centuries to show that this dilemma is inescapable. No idealistic structure can bridge that gulf. In other words, we must die in this world and the next, or "be born again" and partake of God's everlasting life.

Like Nicodemus, the humanist denies the possibility of "re-entering his mother's womb." For him man is the centre of the universe and his destiny is limited to this world. He has a right to live happy and free, as long as he lives. When he suffers, he blames society which is not sufficiently enlightened to give him the health, the comfort and the leisure he requires. His surroundings are alone responsible and all abuses are due to ignorance or bad organisation. This at least is the most logical attitude a humanist can assume before the sufferings of the world, whether in peace or war.

When he blames social conditions or any particular individual or class responsible for these conditions, when he abuses a certain political system and denounces its exponents, he loses himself in a tangle of contradictions. For these individuals or classes, being human and, according to him, good, should not exert such a disastrous influence. The system itself cannot be responsible for the evil it brings about.

Many solutions have been offered to this insoluble problem. They can all be reduced to the argument put forward by scores of writers, from Jean Jacques Rousseau to D. H. Lawrence: "Civilisation is the chief cause of abuse and frustration, for it alters man's true nature. Had he not been compelled by laws and conventions to act against his true instincts and impulses, man would not have developed these defects which make social life so painful." To appeal from human imperfection to nature's presumed perfection leads to disorder and anarchy. Even if it could be proved that the "state of nature" excludes suffering, humanistic philosophy would still be confronted with a formidable question: How and where did the fundamental goodness of Nature pervert the fundamental goodness of Man?

Religion which was rejected as a delusion becomes the only possible reality since Humanism has revealed itself to be the worst of all delusions. Man stands once more at the crossroads. The choice made at the time of the Renaissance has led, not to a new birth or to an earthly Paradise, but to the land of death and despair, the city of Dis. If man is to emerge from the fire, he must recognize at last that there is neither life, light, freedom, nor love without God. The experiment is decisive. Humanism will lead to a last struggle between robots or cease to be Humanism. The choice lies between Christ and the ant heap.

God may be denied, but man and his sinfulness will assert themselves if He is. The meaning of life can be twisted, but death will bring its judgment upon the twister. Joy can be debased, but pain will afflict the debaser. Without the help and grace of God, man's nature must rapidly degenerate into that of a monster: a cunning brute with a twisted soul. Without the hope of eternal life, death becomes the final dissolution of body and soul, the negation of personality, a pit of nameless corruption. Without the joy of eternal life, pain saps the very source of man's strength and drags him down to hatred and ruin. It is impossible to make sense of the universe if we separate the inseparable.

Death and pain belong to human destiny together with life and joy, but they cannot be misinterpreted to the same extent. Life and the joy of life may be exalted in shining marbles against the Grecian sky, or fill the canvasses of Titian and Rubens with a resplendent abundance of nude allegories. Death and pain cannot be idealised. The implacable destiny of the Greek tragedies and the moral conflict of the Elizabethan drama are in the background, while man's passions and ambitions stand in the limelight. It is true that the romantic poets have embroidered some of their most melodious elegies round the theme of death and pain—more particularly the pain experienced by the deserted lover—but their complaint, however sincere, remains the expression of their personal sentiments. As implicit believers in the goodness of man, they are shocked at discovering that all women are not angels or that some lives come to an abrupt end. They deplore these changes and the passing of time, as if they had the right to expect that all women should be faithful and that friends and lovers should never part. They seek refuge in a self-pity which flatters their egotism. The lament echoes from Byron to Lamartine. Shelley writes:

> The flower that smiles to-day
> To-morrow dies;
> All that we wish to stay
> Tempts and then flies.
> What is this world's delight?
> Lightning that mocks the night,
> Brief even as bright.

and Musset answers:

> *F'ai perdu ma force et ma vie*
> *Et mes amis et ma gaieté,*
> *F'ai perdu jusqu'à la fierté*
> *Qui faisait croire à mon génie.*

The novels of the period are full of broken hearts and fainting women, but the women recover in due time and most of the hearts are soon mended. Melancholy is not suffering; it is often an attitude which it may be pleasant and even advantageous to assume—since the melancholy of a romantic man is particularly attractive to a romantic woman. Barring a few exceptions—such as Browning— the romantics talked so much about pain that they seldom experienced it. They grew eloquent on the subject, but did not face the problem which the subject raised. This was the inevitable result of an attitude of mind which could not surmount the insuperable difficulty of reconciling these unexpected realities with a world built on the fundamental goodness of man, from which death and pain had been excluded. The literature of the last century was a literature of disillusionment because it was founded upon an illusion. It was only concerned with one part of life. A stunted reality is like a stunted tree, it is apt to grow crooked.

. . . . .

A reasonable conception of death and pain does not imply the sacrifice of life and joy, not even that of the joy of life, but it implies a conception of the universe in which these realities are considered in their proper perspective.

Whatever device man may use to improve his lot, the fact remains that his life comes to an end and that the joy he may derive from it is balanced by a corresponding amount of pain. The most fanatical materialist cannot escape the menace which threatens him. He may scorn it or defy it, but he must in the end recognize its existence. Death, and the inevitable separation from all he cares for in this world, awaits him at the end of the journey. Pain is his constant companion. Even if he hopes to reduce physical suffering—want, disease and the havoc of war —to a strict minimum, he will still be tormented by moral suffering. No social reform will take away the pang of frustration in love, in ambition, in family and social relations. Complete peace of mind could only be purchased by sacrificing these relations. If holy hermits ever found it, it was because they were favoured with the company of God and His angels. Robinson Crusoe did not discover it on his desert island, and even this somewhat inhuman hero was considerably relieved when he secured the friendship of Man Friday. Loneliness is the most frightening thing in the world.

The first fact to realize if we wish to think clearly about man and the universe is that man's destiny rests on four realities: life, death, joy and pain. Life without death is a drama without conclusion, joy without pain is mere hedonism. There can be no greater mistake than to isolate one from the other and try to avoid a conflict which is the essence of human existence. This conflict is not irrevocable. Unity can be restored, but it can only be restored by God.

"My sheep hear my voice, and I know them and they follow me: and I will give unto them eternal life; and they shall never perish, and no one shall snatch them out of my hand." The early mosaics of Paradise where sheep graze under palm trees, while the Good Shepherd watches over them, are far more faithful to the text of the Gospel than the pictures in which well-known saints may be recognized among the blessed who rejoice in the flowery meadows of Flanders or Tuscany. The Christians are promised reunion with their Heavenly Father. They will be delivered from the "bonds of the flesh," that is of the world and its temptations. All the barriers which separated them will be broken down. They will be brothers in Christ and follow Him wherever He guides them. We are not told what eternal life will be; its true character cannot be expressed in human terms. The more we probe this mystery, the more we realize that it must lead, not to the prolongation of our earthly life, but to the reconciliation of that life to God through death; not to the indefinite prolongation of our earthly joy, but to the redemption of joy through pain. The deliberate effort to choose joy and to reject pain reduces them both to the level of what we call happiness and unhappiness, good fortune or misfortune.

This barrier was once and for all broken down by Divine love and sacrifice, and it is this barrier which Christ urged us to break down in all his words and actions while He dwelt among us, from the beginning of His ministry to the supreme ordeal of the Cross. Whenever we succeed in making our neighbour's pain our pain, and his joy our joy, we approach the Kingdom where death is "swallowed up in victory." Indeed everyone may have experienced that, even in this world, our purest personal joys are not unmixed with pain, and that when we feel supremely alive, we long to give up our life for something greater and better than ourselves. Many poets have expressed this strange exaltation which may be a presentiment of man's ultimate destiny. It is given in the full-blooded enthusiasm of the Renaissance in Othello's:

> If it were now to die
> 'Twere now to be most happy.

and repeated, with a touch of romantic melancholy, in Keat's:

> Yet would you this very midnight cease,
> And the world's gaudy ensigns see in shreds;
> Verse, Fame, and Beauty are intense indeed,
> But Death intenser—Death is Life's high meed.

. . . . .

It is only if we keep these things in mind that we can safely approach the problem of sin and avoid the pitfalls which surround it.

The fact of sin had been recognized, under one form or another, by all religions until modern Humanism reduced it to a defect which was not due to the nature of man but to the circumstances in which he was born and bred. The doctrine of sin is still derided, together with the conception of Evil, and denounced as the superstition of an ignorant age exploited by the clergy in order to terrify their flock into submission. It is pointed out, not without some reason, that a too severe discipline is apt to breed revolt, and that too much insistence on the evil nature of man is likely to provoke temptation instead of preventing it. These ideas have been developed by modern psychologists and have brought about reforms in the judicial and educational systems which have been to a certain extent successful. This, however, only proves that it is better to urge a child or a man to do something good or useful than to forbid him to do something bad or wasteful. It does not prove that the tendency to do these bad and wasteful things is not inherent in the nature of man.

To denounce the abuse of mediaeval restrictions does not show that mediaeval doctrine was wrong, it merely shows that the soundest doctrine may be misinterpreted, which is precisely what the exponents of Christianity have always said. The same remark applies to the fatalistic attitude adopted by certain sects towards sin, which led some thinkers to deny man's free will because they exaggerated the evil in his nature. Such exaggerations, from Tertullian to Calvin, have distorted the problem of evil, but these distortions should not blind us to the essential features of the conflict between Humanism and Christianity.

According to the first, man is essentially good and man-created circumstances are alone responsible for his faults. According to the second, the nature of man, through the fall, has become evil and, through the redemption and the will of God, may become good. He can choose either the way which, in "thought, word and deed," brings him closer to God, or the way which separates him from Him. This free will is granted by God, but man is nevertheless responsible for his own choice. Fatalism and complete freedom are both excluded. Good and evil are inherent in the nature of man, which explains why, in the most favourable circumstances, he has never been able to follow the one without indulging to some extent in the other. Man has nevertheless been given power to further the Kingdom of God on earth. The realisation of this Kingdom corresponds to the realisation of eternal life, through love and sacrifice, accomplished once and for all on the Cross. The gulf between heaven and earth has been bridged. Both the Kingdom of God and eternal life begin now. "Thy Kingdom come, Thy will be done, on earth as it is in heaven," is not the expression of a distant hope. "Whosoever liveth and believeth in Me shall never die" is a plain statement of fact.[5]

Humanism has not always been atheistic, but it is bound to lead to atheism. To exalt man's power over the universe and over his own destiny is to reduce the power of God to that of a moral adviser, and refuse to accept His supreme and final judgment. To ignore sin and evil is to be confronted with the insoluble problem: How can so much suffering be inflicted upon an innocent world? which leads to the absurd position assumed by Swinburne and Baudelaire when they curse a God in whom they refuse to believe.

The Christian view is not only logical, it happens to tally with the facts as we know them: the contradictory nature of man, the conflict which draws him in two opposite directions and the inevitable consequences of retribution.

Retribution cannot always be shown in individual life

[5] In one sense, Adam may be called the first humanist, for he chose "to be as gods." But "as in Adam all die, even so in Christ shall all be made alive" (1 Cor. xv. 22). "He died for all, that they which live should not henceforth live unto themselves, but unto Him which died for them and rose again" (11 Cor. v, 15).

as long as we consider death as its ultimate goal. Many criminals escape human justice and reap the fruits of their crimes in this world. A number of them enjoy the admiration and consideration of their contemporaries, and it is doubtful whether their satisfaction is marred by the reproaches of their conscience, for this kind of criminal generally succeeds in getting rid at an early date of the burden of self-reproach. Christians believe that God is judging us and that we have to account for our sins before a tribunal which is at the same time far more merciful and far more stern than any human court.

But with regard to history it is true to say that few crimes escape punishment. Most collective sins, whether social abuses, acts of oppression, or violations of the code of human decency, have been paid for with interest. It is a summary justice which involves in the same punishment the main culprits and their sometimes unwilling followers, but this justice is infinitely preferable to the permanent establishment of a gross social or international injustice. People talk lightly of the "laws" of history, as if human affairs could be dealt with in the same way as physics and chemistry. The law of historical retribution works in a far more subtle way. It manifests itself through war, revolution, famine and other calamities. It does not only deal with conscious crimes, it also deals with unconscious mistakes due to greed or neglect. It ranges from floods caused by deforestation to wars of revenge caused by faulty peace treaties, from famine caused by lack of foresight to social upheavals caused by bad organisation. No infringement of the natural law passes unnoticed.

This summary justice is not the direct judgment of God, because it does not seem to take personal intentions into account, but it shows that, even in this world, we can see death and pain as the consequence of sin and neglect. Retribution and all the sufferings it involves would scarcely exist in a world which acknowledged the rule of love and wisdom.

The more we wander from the Kingdom, the sooner we bring upon ourselves the terror and devastation of retribution. Each individual has the power to choose the best way, through his free will. Each society, and more particularly each modern society, in which the citizen can express this will, is responsible for its crimes and blunders. Every liability must be met.

The question so frequently asked to-day: "Why does an omnipotent and good God allow such abominations?" shows better than anything else how far we have strayed from the true meaning of the Gospel. It might be justifiable as a jibe coming from a sceptic, like the jibe directed against Christ by the Pharisees at the foot of the Cross: "He saved others, himself, he cannot save." But coming from a Christian, this question implies a complete misunderstanding of the fundamental doctrine of his faith. Since God gave man the freedom of choice, because love cannot be given under compulsion, He also gave him the liberty to choose wrong, and since the creation is so organized that every wrong choice must bring its own retribution, every sin must bring upon the sinner the consequence of sin, in this world or in the next.

By making the wrong choice the sinner has placed himself in the power of Evil, and there is no compromise possible between God and Satan. God, in His mercy, is ready to forgive if and when man wishes to be forgiven. He is standing at the door; our repentance can open it. For it has been closed through the action of an evil force and if it were to be opened from outside against the sinner's will, only another force could open it. In order to prevent retribution, God would have to enforce love and revoke the law of creation.

Our question therefore should be worded in the following terms: "Why does God not revoke the law of creation to prevent the consequences which must necessarily follow individual and collective sin?" Doubt is implicit in the questioner. His attitude is much akin to that of the Jews who asked Jesus to give them some proof of his power, or that of M. Reynaud, who clamoured for a miracle in May, 1940, so that France might be saved. God's supernatural intervention may upset the laws of nature, but they never upset the laws of reason. As long as the world is not prepared through faith to be enlightened and converted by the natural consequences of sin, it would be both unreasonable and uncharitable to alter them and thus to take from man the last chance he may be given to realize the truth.

. . . .

Liberal Christianity is largely responsible for this misunderstanding of the nature of the relationship between God and man. It has so watered down the wine of the Gospel that many Christians are actually shocked when a modern theologian reasserts the forgotten doctrine of divine judgment. Here again, the same process of selecting one part of the truth—the agreeable part—and rejecting the other, has taken place with disastrous results. Just as life and joy were chosen, to the exclusion of death and pain, so love and forgiveness were emphasized to the exclusion of divine wrath and judgment. While, through the pages of the Gospel, the two aspects of Christ's character and mission are evenly balanced, liberal Christians have thrown a veil on one of them or endeavoured so to interpret it as to make it appear as mere symbolical imagery. Once more, one half of the truth has lost its real significance because it cannot be connected with the other half. Divine love has become sentimental because divine wrath has been removed from the picture.

Salvation does not mean entering the gates of an earthly Paradise flowing with milk and honey, it means reunion with God from Whom man has been separated through his sin. Redemption does not mean the advantage which man reaps from the sacrifice of the Cross, it means that through this sacrifice man may, by the grace of God, release himself from the shackles of the world and win true freedom by submitting his will to his Father's will. The resurrection of the dead does not mean that our life on earth may be continued in heaven under more happy circumstances, it means that we shall be born again to a new life, admitted to the Kingdom of God and allowed to devote ourselves to Him.

Looked upon in this light, the tragedy of death and pain assumes a new and deeper meaning. Death remains a cruel separation, a tearing away from relations and friends, a renunciation of the noble and humble objects and occupations which filled our earthly life, but it is no longer an impasse, a final annihilation of body and soul. There is a chance to enter a new life, not necessarily happier, in the sense that we shall obtain in this new life what we did not obtain in the old one, but complete and peaceful, because we shall be filled with the spirit of God and His power, to surrender our love to His love, our will to His will, and thus to attain complete freedom. The sheep will follow their Shepherd.

Death loses its sting, that is to say, its terror. There is between the suffering endured by the Christian and the suffering endured by the humanist this essential difference that the first is fruitful while the second is barren. The humanist is consistent when he says that virtue can only grow in a contented and prosperous society, since he cannot distinguish happiness from goodness. He is driven to despair when he finds his efforts thwarted by overwhelming forces and his hopes crushed by recurring catastrophes.

To the Christian, neither happiness nor unhappiness are essentially good or bad. They are the result of the conflict in this world between good and evil forces which are familiar to him. What matters is not that misfortune should be avoided and good fortune increased, but that both should be turned into Christian pain and Christian joy. "It is not what happens to us that matters," wrote my son a few weeks before his death in this way, "but how we behave under the ordeals which are given us to endure." All depends on what we make of our life's joyful or painful experiences. If they bring us closer to God, we win a victory; if they bring us farther from Him, we meet with defeat. It may therefore be joyful to suffer unhappiness as it may be painful to enjoy happiness, because our joy, as Christians, is not founded on the satisfaction of our selfish desires, but on our hope that, whatever we think, say or do, is pleasing to God. The Love of God is our unquenchable thirst; it remains with us through joy and pain, through life and death.

.   .   .   .   .

Christians should beware of spiritual pride, but they may nevertheless recognize the fact that their faith has prepared them for the worst catastrophes and more particularly for the recent catastrophe of this war. Their recent record of moral resistance to persecution in Europe is comparable to the glorious story of the early Church under Roman oppression. Among the United Nations, most Christians have hitherto overcome the general tendency towards hatred and vindictiveness and the temptation of saying that God is on their side. They have not lost sight of the fact that "vengeance" belongs to God alone and that all men, however evil they may be, whatever crimes they may commit, remain nevertheless brothers, children of the same Father, until the day of Judgment. Neither have they forgotten that the responsibility for the state of mind which created this evil and provoked these crimes is a shared responsibility and that, once more, the effect of retribution must be endured until the time comes when the faults which brought about this retribution may be repaired.

It is worthy of notice that, while most systems and organisations created since 1918, including the League of Nations, collective security and intellectual co-operation, were shattered in 1939, the great movement towards the reunion of the churches which began before the last war has grown under calamity and persecution. The churches are at present the only truly international organisations which have weathered the storm. By the grace of God, men and women belonging to all denominations, classes and countries, whether neutral or belligerent, worship the same God and gather round the same Cross. In spite of the bitterest conflict the world has ever experienced, they are able to endure their ordeal with patience and to fulfil their duties—even those duties which compel them to fight—without losing their faith in their Father's unfathomable wisdom. They are neither made drunk by successes nor shattered by reverses. They are not subject to expediency, but to principles which are independent of the highest sounding political principles. They are given a fortitude which can overcome every defeat because it does not depend on victory. Christ gives them His peace in a world at war, and no pain can shake their indomitable faith that "neither death, nor life, nor angels, nor principalities, nor powers, nor things present, nor things to come, nor height, nor depth, nor any other creature shall be able to separate" them "from the love of God which is in Christ Jesus, our Lord."

VII.

UNDER GOD

I

IN ONE OF HIS EARLY WORKS, G. K. CHESTERTON COMPARES his experience to that of an English traveller who, after wandering over the five oceans in the hope of discovering the promised land, is somewhat surprised when he hears that he has reached Brighton pier. Setting out from England, he returned to England; setting out from Christianity, he returned to Christianity.

My journey has been somewhat different because, instead of starting from Christianity, I started from atheism. My discovery has been a real discovery. I set sail from a dark continent and wandered throughout the world in the hope of finding the Seven Sisters. It was more in awe than surprise that I saw them at last, their white heads raised under the lowering sky, and their feet washed by the stormy sea.

The Christian, in finding his goal, is coming home. The atheist, after his conversion, must undertake another journey. Behind the Seven Sisters lies a country which has hitherto been a blank to him, wide rivers to be crossed, steep hills to be climbed, unknown, forbidding towns to be explored. He has, besides, a new language to learn, new ways to understand, and time is running short. His comfort is that, if he has not reached his goal, he has at least seen the Seven Sisters, the seven cardinal and theological Virtues of Christianity. They were no figment

150

of his excited brain, no idle dream, but seven stern cliffs of solid chalk, overhanging the rolling breakers.

. . . . . .

The first country I discovered in my search for the Seven Sisters was Prospero's island, the land of Dreams. It was indeed "full of noises" and strange beings, unrelated to the world in which I lived. Because I felt unconsciously that they belonged to me, that they were my own creation, I tried hard to believe in them. I could not possibly adapt my life to that of Ariel or Caliban, but I pretended to do so. I even pretended to be one of those spirits who filled my ears with their illusory songs and howlings. I was made drunk by poetry.

The tragedy of every romantic youth is the tragedy of unreality, the tragedy of Hamlet. How far is this melancholy prince alive as he paces up and down the stage? Is not the actor who plays the part impersonating another actor?[1] Is Hamlet really what he thinks he is, or is he not to a great extent the victim of his own imagination? I do not question his sincerity, but it is possible to be sincere while moving in a world of illusions. Hamlet is not only a prey to his dreams, but also to the theories he had built up round them. Having dreamt so much in this world, he is obsessed by the idea that he might still dream in the next. There is no clear cleavage in his mind between vigil and sleep, between life and death:

> For in that sleep of death what dreams may come
> When we have shuffled off this mortal coil . . .

As a young child, Hamlet must have lived his own life.

[1] Needless to say, this remark does not concern the question of Hamlet's assumed madness, unless we argue that he had acquired the art of deceiving others because he never stopped deceiving himself.

All children live in the kingdom of reality; that is why they are so full of wonder. Had he overcome the circumstances which confronted him later, he would no doubt have reached adult age, which does not mean that he would have "behaved sensibly," but that he would have perceived—as Fortinbras did—the reality of the world in which he was living.

Hamlet is the type of humanistic youth because he has no faith to counterbalance his imagination. He does not live in the world of men and women, but in a world of his own choosing. Closing with reality does not necessarily make you a good man, but it makes you a man: it gives you at least a chance of becoming better or worse than you were. It is impossible for us to believe in God, unless we begin by believing in our natural and human surroundings, unless we acquire that sense reality which is the first condition of faith.

. . . . .

The second island which I discovered was the island of Utopia. Having been thrown among men and women, I could no longer be satisfied with spirits. I exclaimed with Miranda:

> How beauteous mankind is! O brave new world
> That has such people in't!

and proceeded to transform these men, including Antonio and Sebastian, into the perfect beings of my former dreams. There was no sin in them, I thought, no disfigurement. They were all beautiful and good, at least they would have been if they had been left alone, free to break all social laws and conventions.

In one way, I was still in dreamland, but in another I had begun to establish some contact with real beings.

They were not what I took them for, but since they existed I was at least compelled to observe their actions and to compare my models with the pictures I had painted of them.

Disillusionment came with the first pangs of suffering; disillusionment about myself as well as about others, for I had neither the power nor the courage to play the heroic part for which I had cast myself. I suffered to see the human idol shattered at my feet, and the weeds covering the pedestal where it stood. And as I suffered, the mist which covered reality began to lift, and I had a first glimpse of what light might mean.

The third island which I discovered was the island of Joy. It was like a small farm in a rich countryside. The house rested on strong foundations; its walls were thick and the roof was covered with a deep thatch. It was warm in the winter and cool in the summer. It stood some distance from the main road, in a lonely spot, sheltered from the wind by a row of fir-trees. Few people passed that way. When they did, at night, they stopped sometimes to hear the singing or to look at the bright table under the lamp, where the farmer's wife ladled out the soup. Some of them would have liked to come in, but the farmer was too absorbed by his family to listen to their steps on the road.

Prayers were said in that house and there were crucifixes in every room. It was a Christian home, like most Christian homes, in which the groans of human pain are drowned by children's laughter, and tolling bells silenced by holiday music; a home in which people receive the blessings of God, without asking themselves what they have done to deserve them, in which religion is supposed to crown the works of man, instead of prompting his sacrifice.

Life was so full in the island of Joy that there seemed

no time to think of the future. It was so precious that its destruction seemed inconceivable. And so, as the clouds gathered on the horizon, I, like many others, hoped against hope. I did not say that the storm would not break, the signs were too evident for that, but I prayed that it might spare my land or at least my home, and I tried hard to believe that my prayer would be granted. It was a selfish prayer, but God, in his mercy, made it less selfish. Fear opened my eyes to many things I had not seen before. I began to listen to the steps of the passers-by on the road, and to voices calling in the night. I began to realize how much all I had received was undeserved, and how I might be called, at any time, to sacrifice it. Behind the reality of life, I perceived the deeper reality of God, the ultimate goal of human striving, the blinding light beside which all light is darkness.

And so, when the storm broke at last, and when our home was struck by death, I knew that this was not the end of all things, that the island of Joy had not become the island of Despair, that when the storm abated, I would still undertake a last journey, through the stormy seas, to find the Seven Sisters, on a distant shore.

II

Not long ago, passing over a bridge in a university town, I overheard two young people hidden in the darkness:

"Do you love me?" asked the girl.

"Under God."

While I hurried away, these words set me thinking. There is nothing new in the fact that a girl should set the pace in the tactics of love-making and force the matter to a conclusion. But there is something new in the boy refusing to take advantage of the impulse and placing the bond of love, from the first, under God's protection and authority.

If the words I overheard were sincere these young people should stand a fair chance of achieving a Christian marriage. Left to themselves, they would run the risk of temporary or permanent estrangement, inherent in possessive love. Even assuming their affection to be disinterested, they would still strive to make each other happy in their own way, and according to their own lights. They might resist the temptation to use each other for their own contentment, but they would scarcely be able to resist the less ignoble temptation of planning each other's future, of trying to force the other to do or to think certain things which would lead to his or her "happiness."

Young married people, if they are unbelievers or do not bring their faith to bear upon their lives, are faced with the alternative of drifting into a loose friendship which will soon disintegrate, or of coming into conflict because their differences cannot be adjusted. The problem is to reconcile the claim of passionate affection with the claim of personality. These claims are almost incompatible if the two partners stand alone. They are perfectly compatible if they stand under God.

The young man who takes the girl who offers herself to him "under God," does not only make a solemn promise to consider the engagement as binding, he also undertakes to consider the girl as a daughter of God, endowed by Him with distinct characteristics of body and mind which combine to make her what she is. He knows that God cares for each of us as persons, and that no man should dare to tamper with God's creation.

If the relationship between these two young people were direct, they might both ignore personal differences and appreciate every circumstance from their own selfish point of view. Satisfaction, for one of them, would mean frustration for the other. But the moment the lovers' relationship becomes indirect, that is to say, is realised in the light of a common worship of God, no change is propitious which is not sanctioned by Him, and does not fall within the law of all Christians. There must still exist mutual influence, but such influence loses its oppressive character; it becomes almost a form of emulation in the service and love of God. There must still exist painful differences, but such differences lose their bitterness because they are no longer subject to the judgment of self, but to the judgment of the common Father.

. . . . . .

Let us suppose that this love comes to fruition and that the married lovers build their own home. To their mutual relationship will be added their relationship with their family. Once more, the problem of personality arises, as soon as the children reach the age of adolescence and begin to re-examine the problems which were temporarily solved for them by their parents. Differences are inevitable, for the wisest father, or the most sensitive mother, cannot forsee how each of their children will develop, and what his reactions will be to the surroundings in which he is placed. For better or for worse, the world changes from generation to generation, and even the soundest experience must be assimilated to become part of life.

Direct contact between parents and children must lead to conflict, either because parental affection becomes possessive, or because every new experience leads the children to form their own conclusions. Parents can only use their authority or their influence up to a certain point. Beyond this point, they must abdicate in order to allow life to follow its course.

Without God's guidance, the home may be broken up. Under God, it is maintained until the children are able to build homes of their own. For Christian parents should respect their children's personality as they respect each other's personality. They should realize that their family does not belong to them, but to God who made them, not masters, but stewards of their children. They should forsee that a time comes when boys and girls are able to fulfil their own responsibilities and must fulfil them according to their own convictions, a time when filial and parental devotion should give way to an equally filial and parental friendship, and when the parents should learn as much from their children as their children have learnt from them.

Life is constantly changing and it is difficult for old people to keep abreast of things. They possess qualities which it is their privilege to use in their family relationships, but they lack other qualities which they may still acquire if they preserve a young heart and an open mind. Abdication is not easy, but it may be made easier by humility. And this humility rests on the knowledge that God uses our children for His own purpose, and that we are with them striving to love and serve Him, as Father of the Christian family, the Church.

. . .

The more we enlarge the circle of our social unit, from the invidual to the family, from the family to the nation, from the nation to the whole world, the more these two words: "Under God," become loaded with significance. The more also the gap between "what should be" and "what is" becomes apparent.

"What should be" is not Utopia, it is the Kingdom of God. If it has never been founded, it is not because it is contrary to the nature of man, like Utopia, but because it has been hitherto beyond the power of man; it is not because it is unreal, but because it is so real that it becomes almost divine—that is, almost beyond human reach.

We can see a boy accepting a girl's love "under God." We can also see a father accepting a son's friendship "under God." These things are exceptional, but they happen now and then. But we can scarcely imagine a society in which all individual and class interests are subordinated to a common spiritual ideal, in which both authority and obedience are the servants of divine Love. We can still less imagine a world in which all nations and races join in a common effort to glorify God in human life. But there remains a considerable difference between Utopia, in which everything is supposed to be good and right, because man's fundamental nature is supposed to be good and right, and the Kingdom of God on earth, in which everything might become better if man surrendered his fallen nature to the grace of God, who is always good. It may therefore be useful to consider the second while it is sheer waste of time to consider the first.

There has been, in fact, a period in history, at least in European history, when a conscious attempt has been made to establish the Kingdom. The striking contrast which exists between mediaeval worship, art and literature, on the one hand, and mediaeval, social and international history on the other, reveals the nobility of the aspiration and the shame of the defeat. That a society and a civilisation which was meant to glorify God should have produced so much cruelty, superstition and lust for power, shows the distance which separates a divinely inspired ideal from a human attempt to realize it. But the mediaeval ideal did not fail only because, according to Chesterton, "it was found difficult"; it also failed because Mediaevalism was never truly Christian. It can only be called Christian, when confronted with other ideals, such as Humanism, which are at the root anti-Christian. The contrast which, for the sake of clarity, we established in the earlier chapters of this book, between Mediaevalism and Humanism, is somewhat arbitrary. There has been a streak of Humanism, of human self-centredness, even in the golden age of St. Louis. And it is because in the Roman Church and in the free cities which flourished in Western Europe at the time, this streak of Humanism was allowed to develop, that a Christian ideal degenerated into a secular Utopia. It is not enough to explain such a downfall by the decadence of the Church. The harm done by loss of faith in God was largely increased by the rising of man's new faith in himself. The one cannot be separated from the other.

. . . . . .

Those who compare modern to mediaeval society unfavourably are often accused of wishing to "return to the Dark Ages." The use of that term in connection with the civilisation of the four centuries which precede the Renaissance need no longer be considered.[2] Neither is it necessary to discuss the dogmatic views on progress commonly held by our fathers. There is no reason why man should not return to a religion which he has lightly abandoned or deformed, if he wishes to do so. But it would indeed be foolish to return to Mediaevalism, if by that we meant returning to the errors and sins of Mediaevalism, as well as to its virtues. Those who hope for a future Christian Renaissance are not wrong because that hope may be remote—all human "hopes," especially that of salvation, must appear remote. They are only wrong if they wish to bring back to life those things which

[2] *See* page 72.

should be discarded or cannot be brought back, as well as those things which should have been preserved.

Through the folly of confusion and contradiction which hides Mediaeval civilisation we can perceive the outline of an international order, deformed in many of its aspects, but distinctly Christian in its inspiration. The people of Europe, and especially of western Europe, were conscious of their religious and cultural unity. They shared the same faith, the same Church, the same style in art and music. English, French, Italians and Germans understood each other, had the same habits and manners, the same code of honour, the same feeling that they were bound to each other by common obedience to the same God. Apart from vast expeditions such as the Crusades, directed against the infidel, wars were restricted, both in space and time, and seldom interrupted the course of trade. Most people were neither seriously affected by them nor intensely interested in them. Armed conflicts were the result of petty rivalries between princes or towns, within the same country, and depended for their conduct on the co-operation of a small number of nobles with their re- tainers. Even the Hundred Years War which, in its last stage, assumed almost a national character, originated in a feudal quarrel. Mass hatred, as it is shown to an in- creasing degree in modern wars, was unknown in those days, not only because nations were only a loose associa- tion of independent principalities, but also because the belligerents never completely lost sight of the fact that they were sons of the same Father, linked together by the same bonds of service.[3]

[3] Cf. H. W. C. Davis *op. cit.*: "For an attack upon a Christian power, it was necessary that some just cause should be alleged. Public opinion, educated by the Church to regard West-Christen- dom as a single commonwealth, demanded that some respect should be shown to the ordinary moral code, even in international rela- tions."

It needed the Renaissance and its humanistic creed, and the Reformation and its outcry against heresy or papacy to break that bond of unity. The growth of capitalism, and the political centralisation which followed, were important contributory causes; but the original cause must be sought deeper, in the soul of the people who had become more and more blind to their common dependence on God, and hypnotised by the desire to impose their will on their neighbors. The love of Man leads to the oppression of men.

Considered by itself, the achievement of Mediaevalism in the international field may be disappointing; it only becomes comforting when compared with the effect of a series of secular creeds on the conduct of international affairs. In the light of the history of the last centuries, there seems no other alternative to-day to further disintegration and the dance of Death, than a return, not to Mediaevalism in its outward aspects, but to the spirit which inspired certain of its manifestations, and particularly the subordination of man's interest to the authority of God. If this spirit succeeded to some extent in bringing about order out of chaos, it was not owing to the very inadequate and unjust institutions and practices prevailing at the time; it was because, in spite of these institutions and practices, it was not totally estranged from Christ. The fact that some good results could be achieved by such a bad system remains the most hopeful feature of European history.

. . . . . .

Taking Mediaevalism, not as a model, but as a signpost, we may reach certain useful conclusions.

The first is that we should no longer place our trust in any kind of humanistic ideal.

Some people contend that the nature of man has deteriorated. This is by no means certain. In many ways man as an individual has improved during the last centuries. He has grown more sensitive to injustice, more eager for information, more critical of outworn conventions. It is society which has degenerated, because millions of men cannot follow the tenets of individual morality, and because neither truth, nor beauty, nor goodness can appeal to large crowds as much as greed, fear and hatred, hidden under the cloak of self-righteousness. When we speak of the herd-instinct or crowd psychology, we mean that the mass and its impulses are very different from the individual and his conscience. This contrast is another symptom of secularism. Just as nations can no longer share the same faith, individuals within each nation can no longer follow the same ideal. The common link in God, in the highest values, has become the common link in Self, in the lowest instincts. The common unit has become the common denominator. In an atheistic world, the rational development of the individual is always defeated by the emotional degradation of the group.

The second conclusion is that we should no longer place our trust in systems.

The ingenuous invention of legal systems, so much favoured in this century, will be as fruitless as the moral education, so much favoured in the last, unless it is founded on faith. A system, such as the League of Nations or Federal Union can only improve international organisation and facilitate international adjustments in so far as those who establish it are inspired, not by a negative fear of war, but by a positive love and fear of God. Societies are not governed by arguments, but by the sentiments behind the arguments. People are not kept in order by their respect for the law, but by their respect and fear of God who inspired the law. It is often said that the League of Nations failed because it was not supported by material force, but it was not even supported by spiritual force. It was never subordinated to the will of God or placed under His protection. It was proudly erected like Babel and, like Babel, it crumbled over the heads of the builders. For a League or a Federation of Nations implies a supernational authority, and there is no authority to which all nations can ultimately submit apart from the authority of God. It was in His name that the Covenant should have been signed, in His name that it should have been administered, in His name that reforms should have been introduced. If this had been done, sanctions might never have had to be applied. But a Christian League implies a Christian world. The problem which confronts the present generation is to discover an international authority, without acknowledging the only Supernational Authority.

At the beginning of the war, we witnessed a wave of enthusiasm for international systems. The pre-war system being responsible for the catastrophe, a new and amended system would, it was believed, prevent its repetition. The fact that the League failed because it was improvised by men who were not ready to accept its liabilities, and administered by men who were still less ready to make the necessary sacrifices, was almost overlooked. It was agreed that if the mistakes of the Covenant were corrected by legal experts, the effect would be the same as that of mending a defective machine. The system which had broken down would "work" at last, and success would be assured.

The campaign of 1940 put an end to these academic discussions and ever since we have been faced with stern reality. There is the secular reality, showing that we cannot fight tanks and bombers with legal documents and that, unless the powers which have the means to oppose aggression are determined to use them to the extreme limit of their capacity, there will be no hope of restoring and maintaining order in the world. This leads us towards a close alliance between the allied nations who, having achieved military victory, are going to control the destinies of the world for better or for worse. The pendulum which swung one way in 1918 is now swinging the other way, and the hope of discovering a new solution or of "mending the machine" becomes more and more remote. For there is no new solution, apart from Christ, and we must choose between the risk of a law which is not upheld by force, and a force or a combination of forces which can only with difficulty be controlled by law; between the weakness of a reformed League or the strength of pacts and treaties. We may try to camouflage this cruel alternative by skilful formulas reminiscent of a former idealism, but the truth is, this time, too obvious to be disguised. A return to power politics may be deplored, but it is inevitable in the circumstances. The struggle against Napoleon ended in a Holy Alliance of the powers who defeated Napoleon. The struggles against Hitler end in another Grand Alliance of the powers who defeated him. It is to be hoped that during the years to come these powers will not abuse their strength at the expense of smaller states, and it is also to be hoped that they will not quarrel among themselves as the danger which they have had to face together is removed. After Vienna, however, and after Versailles, it would be unwise to discount this possibility.

On the secular level of practical politics, the outlook is not comforting. Once more the peace is likely to be lost because errors inherent in man-made and man-inspired decisions may bring about their natural retribution. Unless a miracle takes place—and the present atmosphere is not conducive to miracles—the new "war to end wars" will bring about a new "peace to end peace."

In order to appreciate the difference between the Christian and the secular conception of the future peace, it is enough to compare the "Ten Peace Points," published in December, 1940, with the "Declarations," made in November, 1943, by the four principal Powers, after the Moscow Conference.

The first document includes the Pope's five points on international affairs, and the five points on social conditions added to them by the heads of the Churches of all denominations in Great Britain. It proclaims "the right to life and independence of all nations great or small, powerful or weak." It subordinates all peace terms, including reparations, to "the rules of justice and reciprocal equity," and all peace regulations to the spirit of God "who alone can give life, authority and binding force to the dead letter of international agreements."

The second document deals with military operations, the constitution to be given to Italy and the punishment to be inflicted upon war criminals by appropriate tribunals. It also provides that "pending the establishment of a system of general security, they (the Powers) will consult with each other and as occasion requires with other members of the United Nations, with a view to joint action on behalf of the community of nations."

In discussions regarding the future opinions are divided between those who defend regional pacts dominated by one or other of the big powers, and those who refuse to give up the dream of collective security in which every state would take an adequate share. But whether we take the narrow and more practical view, or the larger and less practical one, we are still faced with formidable objections. We have still to decide who will control the international force which will police the "region," the continent, or the whole world. If several big powers share the authority, the scheme will collapse the moment a difference arises between them. If all the states share the authority, a similar cleavage may arise, every big power inducing or compelling his smaller satellites to side with him.

To these external obstacles must be added internal obstacles. It would be an exaggeration to say that all the governments concerned in the framing of the future peace are strictly democratic, that is to say are subjected to a democratic Constitution. Even if we assumed that they were, these governments could not control public opinion and, as our former experience clearly shows, public opinion in every democratic country is apt to vary. As far as Britain is concerned, it used to be the tradition of British Governments only to commit themselves to a definite policy for the duration of Parliament, since a general election might alter or even reverse this policy. This is still more apparent in the United States. So that the stability of permanent decisions rests on the instability of a changing popular opinion.

The confidence attached to all these plans depends ultimately on the Wilsonian ideal which inspired the foundation of the League of Nations, and according to which every nation would soon recognize that its particular interest coincides with the interest of all. This belief may be true, to a large extent, during a war in which the life of the peoples and their independence is at stake. It ceases to be true, when peace is restored and when former national competitions are bound to reassert themselves. This happened following Versailles and is bound to happen once more, unless we understand at last that internal and external peace must be bought at a heavy price, that it can only be realized through sacrifice, a sacrifice of wealth, pride and ambitions, and through the gradual subjection of all economic and political power to a higher authority which is not of this world.

.   .   .   .   .

In contrast to this dangerous secular reality it is possible to discover a more hopeful spiritual reality. It springs from the fact that the Christian churches have greatly benefited from the persecutions to which they have been subjected, and that a truer understanding of Christian action has been shown among Christians of all churches and nations. It also arises from the progress made in the mission field which is gradually bringing Asia and Africa within the orbit of Christian civilisation. After so many disastrous failures, man may at last lose faith in himself and rediscover his faith in God, strengthened and renewed by recent suffering. There is a growing belief that history is not made of a succession of senseless events, that life is not a tale

> Told by an idiot, full of sound and fury
> Signifying nothing.

Some people begin to wonder whether what happened two thousand years ago may not happen once more. Then, as now, Christians suffered martyrdom at the hand of tyrants. Then, as now, the Gentiles accepted a Gospel rejected by the chosen people. Then, as now, Christians were few and far between, treated as strangers in a world where human power, human efficiency, human pride, challenged the love of God. We are going back, indeed we have already gone back, to the days of St. Stephen, St. Peter and St. Paul. We are so near the end that we are already able to foresee the beginning.

What we hope for is far more important than military victories or temporary settlements between the victorious nations. It is the return to Christianity, a rebirth of man. This second Renaissance is the condition, not only of temporal, but also of spiritual order, for unless we recover the peace which passes all understanding we shall never win any peace which can be understood. The issue is wider and deeper than life and death, happiness or unhappiness, it is nothing less than the salvation or damnation of the human soul.

This Christianity should be the fruit of hope, not of fear. We should do nothing because we are afraid of war. To be afraid of it, as we were afraid of this one, would be the surest way of bringing it about. We should do everything for the love and service of God and because He tells us to spread His kingdom. As this love and obedience grows, armed conflicts may become more and more restricted, and gradually die out, not because Christians hate and fear war, but because they love and fear God, not because Christians suffer from war, but because they rejoice in God so much that no pain can mar that joy.

. . . . . .

The modern humanist has been called "the good pagan"[4] and I should not like to end this book without paying homage to the good pagan's kindness and moral integrity. Most of us have met at least one man of that type and felt that, in spite of his agnosticism, he was far more Christian in his behaviour than many professing Christians. While admiring his noble character, we are, however, obliged to admit that he lives in a dead past. Christian influence on society, although seriously weakened, is not yet dead; the influence of materialism is very much alive. If there seems to be no future for philosophical and political Liberalism, it is because it rests on

[4] Rosalind Murray: *The Good Pagan's Failure.*

the supremacy of a privileged class. Religion may still appeal to a society ruled by the majority, because it combines intellectual and mystical power, but rationalism is essentially the monopoly of the few. It may produce great men, it cannot produce a great society. Whatever the future holds in store for us, it is not the glorification of the individual. It is either the false glorification of the Community or the true glorification of God. The expression "good Pagans," applied to nineteenth century humanists, is misleading because Paganism, as understood in Rome and Athens, was a popular religion. The modern humanist is not a good pagan, he is a philosopher who endeavours to reconcile the most reasonable features of Paganism to the most reasonable features of Christianity. His intellectual attitude is too complex to be understood by the majority or to exert any appreciable influence on international relations.

A society ruled "for the people and by the people" may be compared to the course of a large river which can be diverted into various channels, but cannot be stemmed. Ever since Democracy was proclaimed in the eighteenth century, legislators have been busy trying to build a dam across the river. In the national field, they have framed constitutions; in the international field, they have drafted treaties, pacts and covenants. In every instance, such constitutions and treaties were supposed to be watertight, and to prevent either revolution or war. Practically in every instance in Europe, apart from England and a few small Western States, the dam has been broken again and again and floods have ravaged the land. For good or ill, the masses are by nature impulsive. They may be moved by ambition, greed or even a thirst for sacrifice. They never listen to reason for long.

Ex-supporters of the League of Nations complain that it was never given a chance. According to them, the plan framed by President Wilson, in the silence of his study, was "disfigured by the politicians of Versailles" and wrecked by the petty conservatism of those who clung to the principle of national sovereignty.

The causes of the League's failure lie deeper than that. They are inherent in the nature of Governments dependent on public opinion, in a secular world. There is no doubt that, after the last war, the enormous majority of the people in the victorious nations wished to resume a normal life in peace and security. The general tendency was to go back to the pre-war period as soon as the "nightmare" was over. But the last war was not a nightmare, it was merely the result of another war which had been waged for half a century, under the name of peace, in the economic field of trade competition. The return to unrestricted competition was bound to lead to another outbreak. A few economists and historians uttered a timely warning, but their voices were drowned in the din of patriotic rejoicing. The entire responsibility for the catastrophe had been fixed on the defeated nations, and nothing could deprive the victorious peoples of the "fruits of victory." The suggestion that the sin which was at the root of the conflict was shared by all, to a larger or smaller degree, was derided then, as it has already been derided to-day.

The unrealistic nature of Humanism and its disastrous consequences during the "twenty years' crisis" are still more clearly shown by the emphasis placed on disarmament. Some of its advocates were obsessed by the idea that wars are caused by the vested interests of those who manufacture the weapons of war. Others contended that, since you cannot wage war without these weapons, it would be enough to forbid their production or their use to prevent all future conflicts. In their zeal to whitewash the nature of man, some of these humanists narrowed still further the field of responsibility. They said that the fault rested neither with themselves—this is always assumed—nor with the ex-enemy, but with the guns, munitions and poisoned gases used by themselves and by the ex-enemy. They wished to remove these dangerous things from Europe, as an anxious nurse would wish to remove knives and forks from the nursery. This challenge to common sense, this confusion of cause with effect, was listened to with rapt attention by the same people who would have howled down any orator bold enough to tell them that the real cause of war was neither arms, nor armies, nor necessarily a particular nation, but man's selfishness increased a thousandfold by international competition, and man's refusal to accept the Christian way of life, substituting co-operation for competition, sacrifice for greed, and charity for hatred.

This refusal led to the withdrawal of America from the League, the struggle for Reparations, the Anglo-French dissensions, the occupation of the Ruhr, the Ottawa Conference, the American Tariff Law of 1929, on the one side, and the rise of Fascism and Hitlerism, on the other. Retribution could no longer be averted.

. . . . .

I shall be reproached for denouncing evil without providing an appropriate remedy. I answer that Christianity is the only remedy. I shall be told that the conversion of the world is scarcely practical politics. I shall nevertheless answer that this and this alone is the solution. Of its rightness, I have no doubt whatever; of its practicability, to any large extent in the near future, I have very serious doubts. But unless we establish a distinction between what is practicable and what is true, we shall never be able to think straight. Many authors, when confronted with such obstacles, are apt to alter their course and to adopt some compromise between what should be done and what can be done. Even if I were tempted to follow their example, I could not possibly do so.

For the Gospel is uncompromising. We have been told by some liberal Christians that the instructions given by Christ to His disciples, particularly in the Sermon on the Mount, are "counsels of perfection" which are not meant to be followed literally. This is a complete denial of Christ's constant attitude. He always insists that we cannot serve God and Mammon, and that those who are not with Him are against Him. We are not advised to try to be perfect, if we possibly can; we are ordered to be perfect, even as Our Father is perfect. If we fail, as fail we must to some extent, we sin. But if we struggle hard to achieve what we know beforehand to be impossible, and if we truly repent of our failure, we are forgiven. Our trust in God's mercy should never blind us to the hard fact that the order is a categorical order, and that failure to comply with the order is unquestionably a failure.

What is true of the individual is also true of society. The gap separating the world as we know it from the Kingdom of God is the result of an appalling collective sin. Now that all nations, all races take part in the same life, we cannot even argue that what happens to one nation or one race is no concern of the others. We are all bound together in want or prosperity, in pain or in joy. Considered in the light of the kingdom of God on earth, our task is so great that we would feel inclined to call it hopeless, if despair of God's Grace were not the worst sin of all. We are bound therefore, as Christians, to struggle on against overwhelming obstacles, to be swept back again and again by cross currents which prevent us from reaching the shore, to go on praying and striving in the midst of our agony, until the time comes when all this praying and striving brings down upon us the grace of God, and we receive at last the power to "progress," not in the modern sense, but in Bunyan's sense, towards the goal set before us. Even then, we should preserve our sense of guilt for achieving so little, and our sense of gratitude for the help of God.

I shall also be reproached for escaping into vague generalities at a time when definite proposals should be made. The destiny of the Church of Christ would not be determined by such proposals, even if I were bold enough to formulate them. But a beginning has already been made. The heads of the churches have agreed on certain principles. It seems probable, in the light of recent developments, that the settlement which will end this conflict will contain certain clauses which will not agree with these principles. That will be the testing time. Will the churches make a stand and openly oppose what they consider as an abuse of power or a violation of Christian Justice? Will they once more declare, as they did in 1940, that the spirit of God can alone "give life, authority, and binding force" to human conventions? Will Christians of all denominations and nationalities face the consequences of this action, including derision or persecution? Or will they follow the way of compromise which they have too often followed in the past?

. . . . .

The temptation to compromise in doctrine is strong; it is stronger still in politics. Most Christians are inclined to buy social reform and international understanding almost at any price. Is it not the will of God that people should not suffer from want, and that the abomination of modern warfare should be removed from the world?

We should, however, steel our hearts against this

temptation and remember that no good and lasting result can be obtained if we allow ourselves to be dominated by selfish motives, even by humanitarian selfish motives. The Kingdom is not built for the contentment of man but for the love of God, and the paradox is that progress only brings contentment to man, if it is made in the name of God. As long at our motives remain man-centered, they are tainted with self-righteousness and self-glory. As long as our achievements are purely humanitarian, they are subject to jealousy and greed. It is only when we work for the glory of God, that our work will be truly fruitful, because when the love of men is placed under God, it is subjected to a supreme power which purges it from selfishness. If I love my neighbour for himself, I still expect some kind of reward or gratitude. If I loved my neighbour for the love of God, I should expect nothing from him; and since I expect nothing, there is a faint chance that I may obtain something. That is the strange way in which God works and that is, no doubt, what He means when He says that if we "Seek first the kingdom of God and righteousness," all the things we are usually seeking for ourselves, such as food and clothes, will be "added unto us."

It is therefore neither prosperity, nor even peace that we should seek in this world, but the Kingdom. If we seek the Kingdom sincerely, we may obtain peace and even some kind of prosperity. By the time we receive these indirect benefits, however, we should have reached a stage when such benefits count very little in the light of the love of God, when we only attach value to them in so far as they bring us closer to Him Who, in peace or war, in joy or pain, stands above all these things, ready to give, ready to receive.

Behind the conflict of these two irreconcilable doctrines: Humanism and Christianity, lies the baffling mystery of human destiny. To obtain anything, we must give everything to God. To have life, we must face death for His sake. The humanistic experiment has been to obtain, to invest and to preserve. It has ended in complete disaster. The Christian way is to give, to sacrifice, to lose. It has been abandoned, it could be tried again.

Among the books which I have found particularly helpful in connection with the problem of Humanism are:

A. R. Vidler: Secular Despair and Christian Faith.

D. R. Davies: Secular Illusion and Christian Realism.

C. S. Lewis: Christian Behaviour; Broadcast Talks; The Abolition of Man.

Eric Gill: Last Essays; Autobiography.

Nicodemus: Midnight Hour.

Charles Williams: He Came Down from Heaven; The Descent of the Dove.

J. S. Whale: Christian Doctrine.

George Every: Christian Discrimination.

Jacques Maritain: True Humanism.

Nicolas Berdyaev: The Meaning of History.

A. G. Hebert: Liturgy and Society.

V. A. Demant: Religious Prospects; God, Man and Society.

A. M. Ramsey: The Gospel and the Catholic Church.

Reinhold Niebuhr: The Nature and Destiny of Man.

William Temple: Nature, Man and God.

G. K. Chesterton: The Everlasting Man.

Kierkegaard's: Works, *passim.*